FACE TO FACE

FROM THE TYRANNY OF PRETENCE TO THE FREEDOM OF AUTHENTICITY

DR JOHN ANDREWS

RIVER
PUBLISHING

River Publishing & Media Ltd
info@river-publishing.co.uk

www.river-publishing.co.uk

Cover image credit: Richard Jaimes

ISBN 978-1-908393-96-8

Printed in the UK

Contents

Dedication

Abigail Willow
Our first grandchild.
May you know the Lord face to face and always be free from the
tyranny of pretence.

Acknowledgements

To Dawn, my wife, my love and my friend. Thank you for your relentless support and generous service, and thank you for your patience with me when I've got my writing head on. Thank you for helping me to be a better version of me. You make me look much better than I am. I love you.

Thanks to Steve Campbell for graciously agreeing to write the foreword. As a leader and friend, you have been both an inspiration and a blessing.

To Tim Pettingale for your continued support, patience, guidance and encouragement and to River Publishing for helping to bring my 14th "book baby" to birth.

To the Lord, the Maker of heaven and earth, who stooped down in grace and wrestled for my soul *face to face*. Thank you for letting me see Your face, carry Your name and serve Your cause. I am forever grateful.

Foreword

If I read a book and I know the author, I cannot help but read it with the author's voice in my mind. However, in this book, I heard two voices. One was the dulcet tones of Dr John Andrews and the other the strong yet gentle, unique but familiar, loving though authoritative, voice of the Holy Spirit.

In the church I have the honour to lead, throughout the year we invite a wide range of guest speakers. If we can, we will have them speak at our Leadership Academy as well as to the wider church family. I always ask for feedback from those who have sat under the ministry of the guest speaker/lecturer. John always comes out top in the "favourite speaker" category. The comments range from "he makes complicated stuff seem simple" or "he really knows his Bible" to "I could listen to him all day". Of course, the Academy students do listen "all day" and still they are left wanting more and usually commenting. "I'd never seen that in the Bible before."

What is that attraction? Why the popularity? It's not complicated: John is a gift to the Church. (Which can make it sound so very easy. It is not). The talent must be put to work and honed and shaped and it's clear from listening to John or reading this book that he is someone who is "a worker who does not need to be ashamed and who correctly handles the word of truth" (2 Timothy 2:15).

As the wise man once wrote, "A man's gift makes room for him, and brings him before great men" (Proverbs 18:16). Jesus taught that, "He who receives a prophet in the name of a prophet shall receive a prophets reward" (Matthew 10:41). In other words, we get to see what they see, as they share the gift they are and possess. So, it is with John Andrews. He is a teacher of God's Word par excellence and his ability to teach from a place of revelation, coupled with the dogged hard work he puts in, enables us to see something previously hidden as we experience those "lightbulb" moments that shape our thinking, actions and destiny.

"Authenticity" is a buzz word thrown around to describe what people are looking for in our day and age. I'm not sure it's ever been any different. I've discovered that people are much more able to spot a phoney than we give them credit for. Maybe our thirst for authenticity arises from the fact that there is so much dishonesty on display in the world. In an age of fake news and spin doctors, sound bites and social media, who or what can be trusted? Who or what is the real deal?

This book doesn't disappoint because not only is authenticity a major theme, but it comes from the writing of a man who has clearly learned, or perhaps better discovered, how to be himself. John not only writes with deep biblical insight, which reflects his commitment to properly understanding the Scriptures, but also with openness and vulnerability. As John has so beautifully written, drawing on lessons from Jacob's deceptive actions: "If we have to wear a disguise to get what we want, then what we want is not ours to have!"

Oh, to be set free to be our true selves! As a young man I remember hearing a preacher speak of a friend of his saying, "You'll never catch him off his guard, because he's never on it!" I've met quite a few people who are constantly on their guard, but I've also met many who, by God's grace, have discovered the freedom of being themselves – the true self God intended them to be. John's message of the absolute necessity of living authentically, free from pretence, with integrity, vulnerability and openness is one our generation is craving to hear. Maybe it's never been any different, which is why the story of how Jacob the "deceiver" journeyed to become Israel "the one who contends with God" is an ever-relevant story. As John succinctly puts it, "Jacob's story is our story".

If we can live in the good of the words John has written, learning lessons from the life of Jacob and his family, we will be more completely who God intends us to be. Our search for truth and the authentic will always lead us back to God where we discover He came searching for us all along. God is a God of the first move, the one who takes the initiative. He is the One who looked for Adam and Eve as they hid in the garden, the One who sent His Son while we were still sinners, and the One who came to seek and save the lost.

I was stirred again to ensure I am seeking God's face, which changes everything, and not just His hand which supplies me with so much good. Ultimately, the latter is not enough because we were made for a face to face relationship with God.

Jacob received a face to face blessing from the Lord. This same face to face blessing is ours also in Christ Jesus as "we all, with unveiled face, beholding as in a mirror the glory of the Lord, are being transformed into the same image from glory to glory, just as by the Spirit of the Lord."

All this and so much more is in this thoroughly Bible-centred book. Not many books are like this. Read it, look for His face and listen for His voice.

Steve Campbell
Senior Pastor
The C3 Church, Cambridge UK

Preface

It was William Shakespeare who penned the words in the mouth of Polonius:

"This above all – to thine own self be true,
and it must follow, as the night the day,
thou canst not then be false to any man."

Though these words are true, they are not the whole truth. We live in a world that increasingly sees the need to be true to self as both a right and a virtue, but as we rush to embrace this liberating mantra, Bible wisdom signals to us a note of caution and care. Seeing self through a human lens alone will leave us with a view of self that falls short of our original design, allowing our identity to be shaped by personal preference and desire. When I am the captain of my own soul, then my destiny is vulnerable to ambition, expediency and opportunism; fuelled by a worldview where self alone has the power to decide *who I am* and *why I am here*.

One of the greatest challenges that humans face is that of releasing the right to self-determination, in both identity and destiny, to the higher wisdom and power of the God who made humanity and the universe we inhabit. Born into a world where survival is success, we quickly learn to duck and dive, manoeuvre and manipulate, push and pretend. As we grasp for what we think is best for us, our true God-shaped self is lost and our God-designed destiny is derailed.

This is the story of Jacob, who lived a life packed with incident, glory and controversy. His is a story of struggle, from contending with his twin brother in the womb, to wrestling with the Lord in the grove. From taking what was not his, to surrendering to what was always his. From wearing a disguise before his father and assuming the identity of another, to standing naked before the Lord *face to face*, and being true to both God and self.

It could be argued that Jacob was true to himself, living up to his name in more ways than one as the grasper! But it wasn't until Jacob was true before the Lord that he began to understand who he truly was and why he was here. Only when he stood before the Lord *face to face* in humility, hunger and honesty was *someone* called from within him who had always been there, and a destiny introduced to him that had always been God's plan for him!

The story of Jacob is our story, for if, like him, we will stop grasping for self, a *face to face* awaits that could change everything.

Dr John Andrews
June 2020

Part 1 – The Face of Pretence

Chapter One – The Environment That Shapes Pretence

Genesis 25:19-28

Pretence is not our natural, default state; rather it's a learned defence. Each of us was born as real, honest and authentic as we could be, as we gasped for breath and grasped for life beyond the confines of our mother's womb. We entered the world as our naked selves, uncovered as God originally intended, free to love the skin we were in and to take our place as a unique member of humanity. Before our birth there was no one like us, and no one yet to be born can ever fill our space and shape. How quickly we learn to play a role not written for us and become a person we were never designed to be! How skilfully each of us learns to hide who we are, disguise what we have and deflect the truth of our God-given identity. How easily we succumb to the tyranny of pretence, labouring under its dictates, yet unable to satisfy its relentless demands. Sooner or later we come to the realisation that we cannot escape who we really are. That the person we are pretending to be only exists in a misguided fantasy or unfulfilled dream.

Though Jacob was ultimately complicit with the disguise he worked to maintain for many years, it was not entirely of his own making. He was as much a product of the context he inherited as he was the architect of a mindscape that became the engine room of his behaviour. Environment has been defined as "the surroundings or conditions in which a person operates", and although Jacob came out grasping his brother's heel, he entered a family saturated with emotional ecstasy, spiritual expectation and cultural restraint. Each of these factors on their own was a powerful force, but when they collided together, by default or design, an environmental cultural current was created around Jacob that moved pretence from probable to inevitable. Before Jacob had finished sucking in his first breath, he was welcomed into an environment that was unwittingly conspiring against who he was, thus nudging him persistently towards disguise, as conditions outside of his choice and control worked to shape the person he was and would become.

What helped shape the environment of Jacob's world?

Isaac's prayer

"Isaac prayed to the Lord on behalf of his wife, because she was barren. The Lord answered his prayer, and his wife Rebekah became pregnant." (Genesis 25:21)

The Torah illuminates the situation so clearly and simply that if it wasn't for the other clues in the text, we might get the impression that this is a relatively straightforward inclusion to inform us of the context of Esau and Jacob's conception. But two little chronological inclusions either side of this information open to us the unspoken challenges of holding in tension faith and frustration. Verse 20 informs us that Isaac was *forty years old* when he married Rebekah, while verse 26 tell us that Isaac was *sixty years old* when he became a father to the twins. What the Torah summarises in a simple fourteen-word statement, Isaac and Rebekah took twenty years to live. These boys were a long time coming and their arrival heralded joy for Isaac in the form of his posterity and relief for Rebekah as the stigma of barrenness was removed. Twenty years is a long time to wait, yet Isaac's continued prayerfulness through this experience shows us that faith remained alive, even in the midst of frustrations and disappointments. The birth of Esau and Jacob was the culmination of their hope and the realisation of their faith. They were not merely the fruit of sexual union, but of supernatural intervention. These boys were *special*!

The moment someone (or something) is seen as *special*, we tend to view them through a lens of expectation, which may be greater than the reality itself. We project onto them our hopes and desires, believing they can give us a return, which may or may not be possible. When we become so invested in someone (or anything) in this way, we must be wary of the temptation to make the object of our specialness into what *we* want them to be, rather than empowering them to be the best version of themselves.

Michael Jordan stands out as one of the greatest basketball players of the 20th Century and for some, "His Airness" is the greatest that has ever lived. His list of achievements within basketball are truly staggering, including Rookie of the Year; Five-time NBA Most Valuable Player; Six-time NBA champion; Six-time NBA Finals Most Valuable Player; Ten-time All-NBA First Team; Nine time NBA All-Defensive First Team; Defensive Player of the Year; 14-time NBA All-Star; Three-time NBA All-Star Most Valuable Player; 50th Anniversary All-Time Team; Ten scoring titles (an NBA record and seven consecutive, matching Wilt Chamberlain) and finally, an NBA Hall of Fame inductee.[1]

However, in October 1993, Jordan announced his first retirement from the sport and in 1994 surprised many people by signing for the Chicago White Socks, a minor league baseball team, later being assigned to their major league system that same year.

---

1. https://www.nba.com/history/legends/profiles/michael-jordan

When asked why he had shifted sports at the height of his career, he cited that it had been an ambition of his late father (killed in July 1993), *who had always dreamed of his son becoming a major league baseball player.*

In 1995, after an unsuccessful time in baseball, Jordan returned to play for the Chicago Bulls basketball team where he had previously achieved fame and success, helping them to three successful NBA Championships in 1996, 1997 and 1998, while registering 72 regular season wins in the 95-96 season – an NBA record. His Airness was back where he belonged!

How we are perceived and received by the environment around us can have a profound impact on the person we decide to become, and on the face we choose to wear.

Sometimes we are because of what our world wants us to be, not because of who we actually are.

God's prediction

"The Lord said to her,
'Two nations are in your womb, and two peoples from within you will be separated; one people will be stronger than the other, and the older will serve the younger.'" (Genesis 25:23)

So severe was the behaviour of her babies within her womb that Rebekah, a first-time mum, went to the Lord for advice. The Lord's answer not only revealed the presence of twins, but that the friction within her womb was the beginning of a long struggle that would see the separation of two peoples; where eventually the "…older will serve the younger."

We can only imagine the impact this statement had on Rebekah's thinking, although as we shall see later, it may have influenced her feelings towards her youngest son and eventually her actions on his behalf. From my experience, I know when the Lord has given "a word" or promise over my life, family, church or ministry, I have become susceptible to the two-pronged temptation of trying to work it out and help it along!

God spoke, therefore it will look like...?

The minute a promise is given or a prophecy lands on our mat we usually start trying to imagine when it will happen, how it will happen and what it will look like. Subtly or intentionally we weave our version of God's promise into the fabric of our minds and create an expectation of how it will be outworked in our lives. However, if the Bible (and my experience) has taught me anything, how it was promised and what it eventually looks like can be very different things. Even the speed of its fulfilment and the journey taken *en route* to its outworking can be far from how it was originally imagined. If we are not careful, the expectation we impose onto the promise can create disappointment and disillusionment with the word that God spoke, and the way in which He works.

The Lord told Rebekah that the "...older will serve the younger", but it could be argued that this never happened in Jacob's lifetime. In fact, when the two men eventually reunited after Jacob's long exile, Esau was clearly the stronger in every sense and although Jacob had prospered, he knew he was no match for his brother and that Esau could easily have destroyed him, his family and his dreams. This is reflected in the language Jacob uses:

"This is what you are to say to *my master* Esau: '*Your servant* Jacob says...'" (Genesis 32:4)

"They belong to *your servant* Jacob. They are a gift sent to *my lord* Esau..." (Genesis 32:18)

When Jacob meets Esau face to face, he refers to himself as servant twice (33:5; 14) and to Esau as lord/master five times (33:8,

13, 14 (twice) and 15). It is also striking that in each of these listed references, Jacob refers to Esau as "my" lord/master and as himself as "your" servant, with one exception in 33:14 where he uses "his servant", speaking in the third person.[2]

Eventually, the word spoken to Rebekah was fulfilled and Edom (the older) served Israel (the younger),[3] but in the lifetime of both these men, the older did not serve the younger and the prediction did not materialise as some may have expected!

We must be careful that our expectations are not driving an agenda that the Lord never set or sanctioned.

God spoke therefore I must...?

One of the great challenges for humans is relinquishing control to another. We love to be in control (some of us more than others) and this not only manifests itself in our everyday experiences, it can be a powerful influence on our spirituality too. When a promise comes it is natural to think, "what can I do to help this?" or "what is my part in making this happen?" There is always a tension to be managed between what the Lord has said and therefore what He's responsible for, and which bits we are responsible for. Some promises are clearly conditional: "I'll do this if you will do that", but others, like that given to Rebekah, seem to require no action on our part at all. This is something the Lord will do because He has set His mind to do it.

Giving God a hand has always been a human problem. In a strangely perverse way, we think we can do a better job than Him, or that our wisdom and insight can make the Divine plan work that little bit better! I know you're reading this thinking, "not me", but the

---

2. The words used for master/lord and servant, are the same in all the references. The threads of *'ādôn* and *'eḇeḏ* run throughout.
3. Exodus 15:15, Numbers 24:18, 2 Samuel 8:11-14, 1 Kings 11:14-16, Amos 9:11-12 and Obadiah v18.

reality is we're all vulnerable to this. The Bible shows us example after example of wonderful people who, at times, tried their hardest to derail the plans of God, while all the time thinking they were doing the Almighty a favour.

The record shows that Rebekah thought the Lord needed help to ensure the "older would serve the younger" and hatched a plan that broke Isaac's heart, made Esau mad and almost got her beloved Jacob killed. This is the danger. When we step into the role reserved for the Lord Himself and try to do the parts only He can do, we assume an identity for which we were never designed. The minute we try to make it happen we are into the tyranny of pretence, because we have to convince ourselves and the world around us that we know what we're doing – even though deep down we know that we don't!

We must be careful that our interventions are not creating detours from the pathway the Lord has designed.

When I was born, one of the first comments my mother made when she saw me was, "Look at the size of his feet!" Thankfully, that wasn't all she said. In fact, in the moments that followed, my mother uttered words of prophetic significance over my life. She said, "This boy's feet will travel far and his feet will touch many nations of the world." A few months later at my dedication service, the minister praying over me said almost the same thing, that I would, "carry the Word of God to many nations of the world." Today, in our global village where travel is relatively easy and even the farthest places are within reach for those who can afford it, this word seems unremarkable. But those words were spoken in 1966 when travel, as we enjoy it today, was unthinkable and my parents had never ventured outside of the UK.

Yet, as I write these words, I have had the privilege of travelling to and ministering in 42 countries, and many of those include multiple visits. Every time I get on a plane or step over a border I remember those words; I celebrate the promise of God and the prediction that was made over my life. I've seen the Word of God come to pass in ways I could never have imagined, and without me having to manipulate circumstances, kick down doors or design my own itinerary. The Lord has done it and is doing it, and on the journey I've learned to extract my expectations from the word He spoke and resist the temptation of forcing doors open that He doesn't want opened yet.

Whatever He has promised to you, trust He can do it; trust He will do it in the best way and trust His timing is always perfect.

His promise is not a prison but a picture of His preferred purpose!

Jacob's position

"After this, his brother came out, with his hand grasping Esau's heel…" (Genesis 25:26)

Although Jacob came out grasping his brother's heel, Esau came out holding the golden spoon. By virtue of an event outside of his control, the firstborn of Isaac landed on his feet even though he still couldn't walk. The Law eventually regulated the rights of the firstborn son and with that some safeguards for siblings, but at this moment in history, Esau stood to inherit everything that Isaac owned… and Isaac owned a lot.[4]

Jacob was born into a world where to be the firstborn son was everything and to be second meant reliance on the benevolence of parental generosity. I have no idea how aware Jacob was of his actions as he grasped at Esau, but as we gaze upon those tiny fingers wrapped around his brother's heel, surely we cannot miss a powerful motif, already seen in the early pages of the Torah and repeated often

---

4. Deuteronomy 21:15-17

throughout the rest of Scripture. Humans are rarely content with who they are and under the pretext of self-improvement our actions are often more about self-denial! Jacob was born second, but he wanted to be first. Much later, he would learn that second is first when we know who we are!

To improve self is good, but if that "improvement" is actually a rejection of true self in order to assume a preferred identity, then our motivations are deeply flawed and our actions will take us down a road of never-ending frustration, because we can never truly be what we are not. The Good News offered to us by the Father through the redemptive work of Jesus is not that we become a different person, but that the person we are is made new and re-created, resulting in the best version of self possible – the version the Lord originally intended. The self-denial at the heart of the message of Jesus is not a denial of who we are, but rather a denial of what we want, especially when it sets itself up in opposition to the Lord. The true power of the Gospel is in its ability to celebrate, improve and empower who we actually are, not the person we would like to be.

Jacob was born into a world that not only saw him as second but failed to fully celebrate the fact that he was so. When humans live in an environment where others are celebrated but *they* are not, disguises abound and pretence becomes a friend. In such places our authentic identity can slowly disappear, as invisibility becomes our norm. Hidden in plain sight, our world is robbed of our unique and enriching contribution as we settle for an impoverished version of self.

Second is first when we know who we are!

Parental preference

"Isaac, who had a taste for wild game loved Esau, but Rebekah loved Jacob." (Genesis 25:28)

We don't like to think of our heroes, especially Bible heroes, as being dysfunctional, but it's hard to avoid this conclusion when we read such a text. The family is split right down the middle, with Isaac loving Esau and Rebekah loving Jacob. This is expressed to us in such stark terms that there is little room for ambiguity. However, notice the difference in how Isaac's love for Esau is framed in contrast to Rebekah's love for Jacob:

"Isaac who had a taste for game loved Esau..."

"... Rebekah loved Jacob."

In describing Isaac's love, a rider is attached, namely that Isaac *"who had a taste for wild game"* loved Esau. This translation is a little weak for me, and is better expressed:

"Now Isaac loved Esau because he did eat of his venison..."[5]

Detail is important in the Torah and this insertion shows us that unlike Rebekah, who makes a decision to love Jacob, Isaac's love for Esau was related to the fact that Esau, a hunter, gave Isaac something he enjoyed, namely his game or venison. This is not a case of Isaac loving Esau because he was the firstborn. Rather, he loved his firstborn because of what he does for his father. The problem for Jacob was that he could not compete with this. In contrast to his "skilful hunting" brother, Jacob is described as a "...quiet man, staying among the tents" (Genesis 25:27). Not only was Esau the firstborn, but he was loved and therefore favoured on the basis of his abilities and skills, to which Jacob had no response.

When the giving of love is connected to behaviour it produces a deeply manipulative environment. It puts power into the hands of

5. Jewish Publication Society (JPS)

the one offering love and says to the potential recipient, "In order to have … you must do!" By attaching requirements or standards, love becomes conditional, moving it from a gift to a reward, and transforming it from an instrument of freedom into a weapon of control. Conditions weaponize love, creating a context of forced subjection rather than willing surrender. When those conditions are directly linked to the personhood of the one seeking love, it forces the person either into conformity ("I will do in order to get love") or confrontation ("I cannot do, therefore I am not loved").

Isaac was a good man and probably never set out to do this, but the moment he attached the skills of Esau to his love, he excluded Jacob, because the "quiet man" was not a hunter. Of course, Jacob could have learned to hunt like his brother and the text shows he had a flare for cooking, but that is missing the point. To become a hunter would be to give Isaac what *he* wanted in a son, binding Jacob's identity to that of Esau, and making him a slave to an image that was not his own. Thus, to be loved by his father, Jacob would always have to become someone else!

Are you an environment shaper?

As we've already seen, environment has been defined as "the surroundings or conditions in which a person operates" and perhaps you are one who can shape and influence your environment directly because of the position you hold as a parent, spouse, employer, office manager or church leader?

What environment would you prefer?

One where "skilful hunters" and "quiet men" can be celebrated for who they are and encouraged to be the best version of themselves, or one where quiet men have to learn to become skilful hunters to survive?

Conformity and control are the perfect ingredients for the growth of pretence and a need for disguise, for even good people will become whatever they need to be in order to survive. A spouse will bend, a child will yield, an employee will submit and a church leader will compromise if the environment around them is strong enough and they are desperate enough. We don't want to create a world where it is preferable for someone to become the "Esau" we want, rather than the "Jacob" they are. We don't want to create an environment where love is conditional and where only first is best. And, surely, we don't want to create a place where people exist according to how *we* see them rather than who they actually are!

Wherever I have gone in the world I have observed three common denominators of life giving and authentic, identity-shaping environments:

Acceptance – I love you
When people are loved for who they are and not who we would like them to be, *they thrive.*
Celebration – I see you
When people are celebrated and not tolerated, *they thrive.*
Investment – I believe in you
When people are valued and not used, *they thrive.*

As we shall see in the coming pages, Jacob was no angel, for he willingly wore the clothes of another, lied to the face of his father and stole what was never his. But the actions of this man are not his alone. Yes, he must take ultimate responsibility for what he did, but the power of the environment around him cannot be ignored nor underestimated. In the life of Jacob, a number of factors conspired to produce a potent culture of pressure that even the strong and secure would struggle to resist. As we've observed in this chapter, Jacob was shaped by factors that were largely outside of his making and control, some of which were good, others which were cultural and some of which were bad and even broken. It's easy to judge him for eventually wearing a disguise and doing what he did, but an honest review of his world shows that this was virtually inevitable. What he became is not such a shock when we accept what shaped him.

Chapter Two – The Drivers That Fuel Pretence

Genesis 25:19-34

As observed in the previous chapter, the power of our environment can have a dynamic impact on who we chose to be at any given moment. All of us succumb to the pressure of what is around us, even though our actions are at odds with what is within us. We cannot and should not ignore these environmental factors, but a Bible worldview seeks to focus our attention, and with it our responsibility, on the *IN*vironmental drivers that ultimately fuel our actions and shape the person we are. Solomon urges us to "guard" our *in*vironment (*our hearts*), because the issues of life spring from it[1] and Paul confirms this powerful idea when he concludes that we are "transformed" by the "renewing" of *our minds.*[2] For both men, the internal mindscape has the power to shape external landscape and it is coming to terms with this reality that can produce clarity in our thinking and authenticity in our expression.

Jacob deserves our sympathy, for he entered an environment shaped by deep-seated hopes and motivated by forceful ideas. However, there was a difference between the world the baby was born into and that which the man accepted and embraced. Over the former he had no choice, a subject in another kingdom, but as he grew he had the

1. Proverbs 4:23
2. Romans 12:2

power to either accept what others wanted of him or become the man the Lord intended him to be. Throughout his story Jacob makes choices, which demonstrate that just like us, he was subject to desires and ideas that fed his insecurities, creating moments of desperation and vulnerability within the relationships and the community he was a part of. Jacob's actions cannot be laid at the feet of Isaac, Rebekah and Esau alone, for their environmental influence cannot exclusively carry the blame for what happened next. Rather, Jacob's actions are fuelled by powerful internal drivers suggesting that, in his own eyes, he is not enough and he must be more! As Solomon reminds us:

"Even a child is known by his actions, by whether his conduct is pure and right." (Proverbs 20:11)

What might Jacob's actions *suggest* to us?

Acceptance – "I need"

"Isaac… loved Esau…" (Genesis 25:28)

The moment it became clear to Jacob that Isaac loved Esau, he knew that (in his father's eyes at least), he was different – living in a place of exclusion from the primacy of his father's love. Of all the people who should have known the potential devastation of divided love and loyalty it was Isaac, having been raised the "son of promise" and seen the sending away of his half-brother Ishmael. Accepting that he and Ishmael were brothers from another mother, the pain borne in the heart of the first Patriarch, Isaac's father, is clear in the Torah for all to see. If being "more loved" by his father caused distress in a family already divided, what could such an action produce in the life of a son from the same womb as his brother, but now seen as "less-loved"? There is no indication in the text that Isaac did not love Jacob, but it is brutal in exposing where the focus of Isaac's affection lay. Could this have been an influence on why Jacob was so keen to buy the birthright from his brother? Could this be a factor in why

Jacob risked everything and, in an act of treachery, declared himself to be Esau before his blind and aged father?

We will look at both these events later in a little more detail, and although we must avoid reading into the text something that is not there, we should not ignore a piece of information given to us as a precursor to these events. Jacob's behaviour must be understood, to some extent at least, in the light of this stark truth: "Isaac… loved Esau…"

Acceptance is defined as, "the process or fact of being received as adequate, valid or suitable…" The need for validation lives in all our hearts and everyone reading this book has experienced the joy of being part of, and the pain of being excluded from, a relationship, a family or some sort of community we longed to be a part of. *Being in* feels good, but finding ourselves on the outside of something we want to be on the inside of can create devastation and desperation in us. The pain of exclusion can open us up to the lie that acceptance is everything and therefore anything is justified to achieve it – even if it means sacrificing the truth of our identity and the authenticity of our personhood. When acceptance is a key driver for an individual, anything is possible and everything becomes permissible. When this idea influences our mindscape, good people find themselves doing things they swore they would never do.

Take a moment to reflect on the following questions:

Is there a person or a group from whom you long to have acceptance?

Why are you being excluded?

What is the cost of that acceptance? What is being asked of you?

Do you have to disguise the person you really are to be accepted as the person they want?

Is it worth it?

Acceptance is a normal, natural and necessary part of life, but if to attain it we must hide who we are and pretend to be someone else, then the reward it offers will never truly satisfy us. We may need acceptance, but we also need to be true to our God-shaped self and the call of His design and destiny for our lives.

Loyalty – "I must"

"… but Rebekah loved Jacob." (Genesis 25:28)

Unlike the condition attached to Isaac's love for Esau, Rebekah's love for Jacob is stated in clear simplicity. The text does not suggest that it was in response or even retaliation to Isaac's favour for Esau, or that she didn't in fact love Esau. Whatever the reason, her love for Jacob was obvious to all. Being loved by his mother, in what seems like a polarized context, would have assured Jacob in some way (though I suspect never fully satisfied what he wanted from his father), but also engendered deep loyalty to his mother.

Loyalty is defined as, "Giving or showing firm and constant support or allegiance to a person…" It is generated through investment, developed through trust and earned over time. We cannot demand loyalty from another, rather it must (by definition) be a gift we receive, freely and willingly given. Loyalty can call out of us actions that are both noble and ignoble, and behaviour that is both glorious and despicable. Loyalty has inspired humanity to greatness and led us to debasement!

When Rebekah sent Jacob into his father to steal his brother's blessing, Jacob knew it was wrong. Concerned that he might be caught in this act of deception, Jacob complained:

"... I would appear to be tricking him and would bring down a curse on myself rather than a blessing."

Rebekah's response was uncompromising in its demand:

"My son, let the curse fall on me. Just do what I say; go and get them for me."

The Torah concludes;

"So he went and got them…" (Genesis 27:12-14)

Note in the exchange that even though Jacob knew it was wrong, he yielded to his mother who had played the ultimate loyalty card: "Just do what I say…" In other words, "Trust me, I know what I'm doing." Jacob demonstrated allegiance to his mother in a moment when he should have said no and stepped back from her scheme.

Why didn't he say no? There's no hint that Jacob feared Rebekah and therefore simply did what he was told. His argument with her backs this up. Some may suggest that Jacob did it because of parental authority, and although this cannot be ruled out, we should remember that Jacob was approximately forty years old when he stole his brother's blessing. Could it be that he obeyed out of pure loyalty to her, a loyalty generated over years of relentless love? Is this why the Torah tells us "... but Rebekah loved Jacob"? Could it be that Jacob wore the disguise and pretended to be Esau for no other reason than loyalty to the mother who had loved him so relentlessly? Out of loyalty Jacob wanted to please his mother and was prepared to do something he probably never imagined himself doing.

Take a moment to reflect on the following questions:

Have you ever said yes to something out of love or loyalty that you wish you had said no to?

Are you involved in any relationships (family, business, church) where you cannot say no?

Is your loyalty being used as a tool of manipulation against you?

Anyone who knows me, knows that I am a deeply loyal person. My upbringing was a shaping factor in that worldview, but as a person I have come to know the power and blessing of love and loyalty expressed in a way that enhances and empowers those they touch. For this reason, I remain deeply committed to keeping loyalty a feature of my world. However, I've also come to recognize that my desire to be loyal can be exploited and used by those who understand its power but fail to respect its purpose. Where I have sensed this, and with it a threat to my God-shaped identity and God-designed purpose, I have learned to say no – even to "Rebekahs" I love. Over the years, *no* has cost me friendships, opportunities and in some cases reputation, but I was able to say *no* because I had a stronger *yes* – a *yes* rooted in my identity in Christ, fed by His Word and framed in His purpose.

What if Jacob had said no?

What if confidence in the person he was had caused him to reject the person he was being asked to be?

Sometimes saying yes to the Lord will mean saying no to those around you. Loyalty to Him trumps all other calls over our lives, but when we say yes to Him, we'll never have to wear a disguise!

Significance – "I want"

"First sell me your birthright." (Genesis 25:31)

Esau came in from the fields probably after a hunting expedition, hungry and ready to eat. His brother Jacob just happened to be cooking. Esau made a simple request, but Jacob's response is both startling and shocking.

"First sell me your birthright."

The price placed on the table for a simple bowl of stew represents the culmination of a lifetime of ambition and the crystallisation of Jacob's desire for significance. The grasping baby has now matured into a scheming man. What looked cute and coincidental when the boys were born, has now incarnated into naked ambition. The birthright (*bekhorah*) was the special privilege designated to the firstborn of any father. In some cases, this primacy meant the inheritance of everything the father owned. We see this in Isaac's own experience with Abraham. Even though Abraham had other children the Torah tells us,

"Abraham left everything he owned to Isaac…"

Although it is quick to add that he,

"… gave gifts to the sons of his concubines and sent them away from his son Isaac…" (Genesis 25:5-6)

Later, guided by the Law, this was generally expressed in granting a "double portion" to the *firstborn male* over all the other males in the household. This meant that if Isaac was to follow the same pattern left by his father, then Esau would inherit a huge estate and great wealth. It is hard to imagine that Isaac would not have made provision for Jacob, but whatever was provided was down to Isaac's discretion at the time.

That said, I'm not sure the issue was one of *inheritance* and *money*; I suspect it was about *right* and *position*. Wealth was certainly part of the birthright package, but being the firstborn also meant leadership over siblings after the death of a father. Jacob wanted to be *first* and although chronologically this was impossible, legally he could make it happen… as long as Esau sold him the birthright. Jacob's drive for significance was suddenly unleashed in an audacious act to take his brother's position and finally be first!

Significance is defined as "the quality of being worthy of attention: important…", but how "worthy of attention" and "important" are defined determines so much in the hearts of those who seek them! So many find themselves in a world where significance can only be achieved by aligning themselves with someone else's definition of "important". Thus, in order to be worthy of attention, pretence is normal and a disguise is essential. If *bekhorah* is the standard to which significance is set, then we are forced to pursue and attain the birthright by hook or by crook, and we are slowly squeezed into becoming someone we are not!

The desire for significance in its purest form can be a good thing, empowering us beyond the definitions and limitations set by a world determined to keep us in our place for the enrichment of theirs. But the drive for significance alone, without an understanding of our God-shape and God-call, without the realization that we are not alone and that our journey is bigger than us, can expose us to the tyranny of selfish ambition and self-promotion. Even if, ironically, in seeking something for self we lose ourselves in the process.

Take a moment to reflect on the following questions:

How would you define significance?

Is someone else's definition of "worthy of attention" or "important" determining your behaviour?

Is there a *bekhorah* in your world that you need to be free from?

Until this moment, Jacob looked like a normal young man getting on with his life, but the audacity of this request revealed a smouldering ambition to be more than he was, perhaps because he was not at ease with the man he was. This was not an attempt to improve himself but rather lose himself. Though born second, he wanted to be first!

Opportunism – "I can"

"Look, I am about to die," Esau said. "What good is the birthright to me?" (Genesis 25:32)

Esau's response to Jacob is infamous as one of the most short-sighted, stupid statements in the whole of the Torah! His immaturity is brutally exposed as his selfishness places in jeopardy his whole future. He contemplated the unimaginable: to surrender his *bekhorah* for a bowl of stew. It was the equivalent of selling a multi-billion pound fortune for a Big Mac and Fries (let's go large shall we?!) Yet, incredibly this is what he did. The passage concludes:

"So Esau despised his birthright." (Genesis 25:34)

What Jacob craved, Esau disrespected and despised. Thus was created the perfect opportunity for a take-over – a moment of which Jacob took full advantage. So profound is this moment that the New Testament makes comment when the writer to the Hebrews concludes:

"See that no one is sexually immoral, or is godless like Esau, who for a single meal sold his inheritance rights as the oldest son. Afterward, as you know, when he wanted to inherit this blessing, he was rejected. Even though he sought the blessing with tears, he could not change what he had done." (Hebrews 12:16-17)

What is striking here from a New Testament perspective is both the language used and the commentary given. We get an insight looking back that isn't immediately obvious when we read the Genesis text. Three phrases stand out: "sexually immoral", "godless" and "sold". All three ideas combine to build a damning picture of Esau's state of mind with regard to his birthright.

Let's look at them a bit closer before returning to Jacob.

"Sexually immoral"

There's nothing in the Torah that explicitly points to Esau's behaviour in a sexually immoral way, so why this comment, specifically in relation to this moment? The word used here is *pórnos* which comes from *pernáō* meaning "to sell". In the Greek world, someone who prostituted himself for gain was classed as *pórnos*, hence its association with prostitution and sexual immorality. But look how the writer to the Hebrews uses it in the context of Esau, highlighting the fact that although Esau did not act in a sexually immoral way, he sold something in an inappropriate or sinful way – a birthright that was both precious and valuable!

"Godless"

Linked to this idea is the word "godless". The word used in the text is *bébēlos,* derived from *baínō* (to go), and *bélos* (a threshold). This phrase came to signify a person who was (or should have been) barred from crossing the threshold of a temple. Hebrews is making it clear that when Esau made his decision he never once considered God in the equation and did not pause to think, "What does the Lord want in this moment?" Instead, his actions were completely and entirely self-centred, thus rendering them *without God* – godless!

"Sold"

The word used here is *apodídōmi* from *apó* (from) and *dídōmi* (to give). Esau exchanged his birthright and put a price on something that others may have regarded as priceless. What should never have been for sale was placed on the table, not by Jacob's offer, but by Esau's agreement. Had Esau realized what he had, no amount of stew would have moved him to sell. The issue at the heart of the sale was not how good Jacob's stew was, but how little Esau valued his *bekhorah*!

So, it's Esau's fault, right? Well, yes and no. Our journey centres on the story of Jacob. The tragedy of this episode is that it not only exposed Esau's obvious stupidity, but Jacob's ruthless opportunism. Jacob took full advantage of his brother's weakness and confusion. Nowhere in the story do we see Jacob showing compassion, offering counsel or urging caution to his older brother. If we did not know they were brothers and we stumbled upon this conversation, we might think of them as two business adversaries bartering for supremacy.

Some will read this text and say Esau deserved it for his ineptitude; that this is but the beginning of the fulfilment of the prophecy that the "older will serve the younger". But, we must be careful not to allow the end to dictate the means or to lightly surrender our principles to the mercy of pragmatism. At one level Jacob did nothing wrong in offering to buy his brother's *bekhorah*, but at another, Jacob exploited the vulnerability and weakness of his brother in such a way that an honest transaction felt like daylight robbery! In the light of the comments of the writer to the Hebrews it seems reasonable to ask whether in fact Jacob encouraged Esau's immorality and godlessness. Though Esau must take responsibility for his own actions, wasn't Jacob an enthusiastic provocateur in his brother's misadventure?

The dictionary defines an opportunist as, "a person who takes advantage of opportunities as and when they arise, regardless of planning or principle". Is this not a definition of Jacob as seen in our story thus far? But the opportunism seen here is but the fruit of a mindscape that has been shaped by the "I need" of acceptance, the "I must" of loyalty and the "I want" of significance. Opportunism is not the product of random coincidence, but rather the inevitable expression of ambitious desire. With such a powerful concoction at the heart of any human, the question is not "will it happen?" but rather "when?"

Remember:
God-created opportunities will have God at the centre – opportunism places self at the centre.

God-created opportunities will always be bigger than self – opportunism is all about self.

God-created opportunities keep truth foundational – opportunism allows truth to become optional.

God-created opportunities will bring blessing to those around us – opportunism uses those around us.

God-created opportunities enlarge our world – opportunism shrinks it.

Take a moment to reflect on the following questions:

What is more important to you, personal advancement or principles and values?

Is there an *Esau* in your life that you're taking advantage of in order to promote or benefit self?

Are you prepared to look for the God-created opportunity, even if it means a longer wait or a different route?

As a follower of Jesus, I believe in the Lord of opportunity. The Word of God counsels me that if I trust Him and place His wisdom above my own, He will make straight paths for me, opening doors that no one can close and closing doors that no one can open. Belief in the God of opportunity delivers me from dangerous opportunism, which places the promotion of self at the centre, leaving me open to compromise and corruption. I have discovered that any opportunity the Lord creates for me will not involve the abuse, manipulation, exploitation or corruption of another, regardless of their own ineptitude, for I will never have to destroy another's dream to get to where the Lord wants me to be.

Shaped by a mindscape where the *I need* of acceptance, the *I must* of loyalty, the *I want* of significance, and the *I can* of opportunism form our worldview, our true identity will be under relentless pressure to succumb to what others want from us or what we think might work. These ideas lurk at all our doors, hoping for entry and ultimately permanent residency within us; to establish themselves as strongholds in our thinking, which over time shape us into someone other than the person we were created to be. We must remember, *second is first when we know who we are!*

Chapter Three – Rebekah: Accepting Another's Dream

Genesis 27:5-17

Though this is Jacob's story, Rebekah his mother played no small part in the making of this particular moment. It is her hand that seems to guide the events in question, and her plan that sometimes forcefully, sometimes subtlety, shapes the behaviour and responses of the men she loved. Isaac was the Patriarch of the family but Rebekah is the protagonist of the story. As such, she significantly influences the direction of her youngest son and, beyond that, the destiny of the nation within him. The meaning of Rebekah's name (*Rivqah* or *Rivka*), is not obviously clear, but it is suggested that it points to the idea of "tying something" and of "fastening or securing", such as a calf in the stall, for example. Interestingly, in Arabic the name points to a "rope with a noose".[1] Whether she knew it or not, the wife of Isaac and mother of Jacob lived up to her name. She left nothing to chance, ensuring that her hopes for the son she loved were realized. Through her actions, she "fastened" Jacob's destiny to her desire!

---

1. The root of this noun and the name is רבק, which is not found in the biblical text. However, this root is found in other Semitic languages and means "to tie fast" or "secure", just as a calf is "secured" in the "stall". https://www.ancient-hebrew.org/names/Rebekah.htm

As alluded to in a previous chapter, Rebekah openly manipulated Jacob into doing something that he knew was both wrong and dangerous. But she also manoeuvred Isaac without his awareness, so that he became party to her scheme and a supporter of her plan. Both Jacob and his father ended up doing what she wanted and willingly, or unwittingly, found themselves accepting another's dream. Rebekah demonstrated that even strong minds can be influenced and strong wills moulded.

But why was Rebekah so driven in this direction; so determined to execute her plan? Just as Jacob was shaped by his environment and fuelled by his *in*vironment, his mother's actions were not random and incongruent, they were an expression of all that was within her and all that she wanted. It seems Jacob wasn't the only grasper in the family!

Shaped by what she heard

"… the older will serve the younger." (Genesis 25:23)

Though the older would not serve the younger in the lifetime of her two sons, Rebekah was not to know this, and she was undoubtedly shaped by the word the Lord spoke to her. There are theories that these words may not have meant what they appeared to mean, but the actions of Rebekah suggest that what she heard was straightforward and clear: Esau would serve Jacob![2]

It is inconceivable to think that Rebekah was not shaped and influenced by this word, and though there is no hint that it dominated the early lives of her sons, it would not have been far from her thoughts. The word was "treasured in her heart", making her mindful in every conversation and interaction within her home.

2. Rabbi Jonathan Sacks, *Covenant & Conversation: Genesis – the Book of Beginnings*, Maggid Books, 2009, pp.153-157

Could it be that Rebekah saw herself as the guardian of this word and saw in her own journey a measure of responsibility in seeing it come to pass? Though the Word was about the destiny of her sons, did she somehow become "fettered" to it and drawn into the drama of its fulfilment? After all, the Lord spoke the promise to her!

As beautifully summarized by Sacks, "The present is never fully determined by the present. Sometimes it is only later that we understand now... We live our lives toward the future, but we understand our lives only in retrospect."[3]

The Torah doesn't give us Rebekah's retrospective understanding of these events and so we have no idea if what she eventually understood differed from her understanding in this moment, as the story played out before her. However, there can be no doubt that how she heard and interpreted the word the Lord gave her, framed how she saw her sons and thus her behaviour towards them.

When it comes to the word of the Lord to us, whether it comes directly to us as it did to Rebekah, through the Scriptures, or through a man or woman of God, we must be careful to address two vital questions:

What did the Lord *actually* say?

It is so easy to hear what we thought He said or, worse still, what we hoped He said. As humans we are vulnerable to interpret things in our favour and to hear them in the light of our worldview. It is always gratifying when what the Lord says affirms our ideas and aligns to our desires. This is so ingrained within us that most of the time we're not even aware that it's there. But often our ego, prejudices and passions are at work, manipulating His word into what we want.

---

3. Sacks, *Covenant & Conversation, Genesis…* pp.155 & 157

What does this mean?

The meaning of His word to us will only be clear if we're open to what He actually said. Sometimes when the Lord speaks a word to us it's immediately clear what it means. But there are times when it's not clear … at least, not yet. It is in these moments that we must be careful, humble and courageously cautious. When there is lack of clarity around God's promise, it requires an expression of faith. We have to trust Him with the detail, thus enabling us to relinquish control and avoid the risk of making His word mean something it may not mean.

In Luke's Gospel, Mary the mother of Jesus is confronted with two words that she did not understand. The first was from Gabriel, who tried to explain to her how Jesus would be born through her. Note her reaction:

"I am the Lord's servant, may it be to me as you have said." (Luke 1:38)

Years later, when Mary and Joseph eventually find the boy Jesus at the Temple after frantically searching for Him, He explained to them His behaviour and the text explicitly concludes that they did not understand, but Luke offers this beautiful conclusion:

"But Mary treasured all these things in her heart." (Luke 2:51)

The word translated "treasured" is *diatēréo¯* which points to the idea of "guarding" or "watching over" something. She protected the words even though she didn't fully get their meaning. When she didn't understand the word of God, she *trusted* and she *treasured*!

Take a moment to reflect on the following questions:

If the Lord has spoken to you… what did He actually say?

Is it possible you have added meaning to His word that wasn't there?

Are you willing to trust Him in the ambiguity of His promise?

Impacted by what she saw

Genesis 26 records an episode in the lives of Isaac and Rebekah where Isaac takes matters into his own hands – the consequences of which must have impacted his wife.

"When the men of that place asked about his wife, he said, 'She is my sister,' because he was afraid to say, 'She is my wife.' He thought, 'The men of this place might kill me on account of Rebekah, because she is so beautiful.'" (Genesis 26:7)

The actions of Isaac toward Rebekah are startling, whatever the cultural context, but the verses preceding these actions make them even more remarkable. Genesis 26 begins by telling us that there was famine in the land, followed by a direct word from God to Isaac:

"Do not go down to Egypt; live in the land where I tell you to live. Stay in this land for a while, and I will be with you and bless you…"

The encounter concluded:

"So Isaac stayed in Gerar." (verses 2-6)

The echo of Isaac's situation and his father's earlier experience is unmissable in the Torah. In Genesis 12, Abram arrived in the land of promise, only to encounter famine. He then left for Egypt and it was there that he asked Sarai to lie for his own safety:

"Say you are my sister, so that I will be treated well for your sake and my life will be spared because of you." (Genesis 12:16)

Instead of leaving for Egypt, Isaac is told explicitly by the Lord not to go there and given a powerful promise from the Lord of both His presence and prosperity. Protection was certainly implicit within the promise! Yet, in spite of this word, Isaac followed the exact same pattern of his father, with the exception that he did not ask Rebekah to lie for him. He lied instead! "She is my sister…"

A pragmatist is defined as someone "guided more by practical considerations than by ideals". Without being unkind to Isaac, this is a perfect description of his mentality at this moment. Even though the Lord had spoken to him, he took matters into his own hands in order to get what he deemed was best for him. For Isaac, the end justified the means, regardless of what the Lord had said or the impact of his actions on the woman he loved. Rebekah is at the epicentre of this intrigue and witnessed first-hand the behaviour of her husband in the light of the word God gave him. After all, "all is fair in love and war", and this was not only a fight for survival – at stake was God's promise of land and descendants. Isaac believed himself justified in his actions, because the Lord was with him!

We can only surmise what impact such an episode had on Rebekah, although the Torah remains silent on these details. However, is it possible that the pattern she saw at work in her husband became the blueprint for her own behaviour towards her sons? Like Isaac, she received a word. Like Isaac, could she have concluded the end justified the means, even if that meant deceit and betrayal? This conclusion may be an uncomfortable consideration, even a step too far, but the link between the two episodes, however tenuous, cannot be ignored. Rebekah may not just have been at the rough end of Isaac's pragmatism; there is a strong possibility she actually learned from it and copied it!

The impact of our example usually outlives the echo of our words. People can forget the details of our words relatively easily and quickly, but what they see, feel and experience in the example of our behaviour carries longevity, regardless of the legitimacy of our actions. How we "do the word" carries more weight than how well we quote it.

We must resist the temptation lurking within us to allow pragmatism to drive purpose. When practicalities eclipse principles and ideals, the purposes of God are at the mercy of our whims and desires. Behaviour that gets us what we want trumps the attitudes within us that the Lord wants, and as we pursue a pathway where the end justifies the means, anything becomes possible – even the most improbable!

Take a moment to reflect on the following questions:

Can you think of people in your life who have created a good example by modelling the word of God well?

Are you tempted to allow the end to justify the means? If so, why does this happen?

Is there a 'Rebekah' in your world who saw an example for which you should apologise and ask for forgiveness?

Motivated by what she felt

"… Rebekah loved Jacob." (Genesis 25:28)

We considered this statement in Chapter One, although from a slightly different perspective. As we try to understand Rebekah's impact on the story, and the motivation for her actions, this statement must be at the heart of why she works so hard on Jacob's behalf, at the expense of Esau. There is no clear statement in the text that even implies Rebekah did not love Esau, in fact, something of her own pain comes through. Towards the end of the story it records:

"Why should I lose both of you in one day?" (Genesis 27:45)

However, as Esau became a man, his actions made it easier for Rebekah to prefer Jacob, encouraging a growing sense of prejudice towards her youngest son:

"When Esau was forty years old, he married Judith daughter of Beeri the Hittite, and also Basemath daughter of Elon the Hittite.

They were a source of grief to Isaac and Rebekah." (Genesis 26:34-35)

The word translated "grief" here is *mōrāh*, meaning "grief" or "bitterness". It can describe an emotional response to disappointment or sorrow of spirit over an incident or issue. Even before we enter chapter twenty-seven where we see Rebekah's plan in full flow, a dangerous and divisive emotional concoction is brewing – namely love for her youngest son and disappointment in her eldest. Such powerful feelings might only fuel the sentiment that Esau doesn't deserve the blessing, while Jacob clearly does!

As we observed in Chapter One, love became weaponised when conditions were attached to it. Now we see love becoming one-sided and distorted because comparisons have been attached to it. Just as Isaac's love for Esau (with his taste for wild game), created a detrimental comparison between his sons (to Jacob's disadvantage), now the same destructive cycle of comparison is turned to Jacob's advantage by Rebekah. Her delight in Jacob is made stronger and more focused because of her disappointment in Esau. What she heard collided with how she felt about both her sons, surely confirming her conclusion that the older *must* serve the younger.

Sometimes we have to have the humility to admit that it is our feelings not our faith that motivates some of the decisions we make. Feelings and emotions should not be ignored, but the journey of faith calls us to manage them with integrity and an openness and honesty of heart. When it comes to making significant decisions about our own lives or those we are influencing, "I just feel…" cannot be the only word and should not be the final word. When what we feel is so predictably unpredictable, we must not lean too heavily on emotions that can be manipulated by comparison, disappointment, chemistry or conflict. Over-indulging our feelings will grant emotional justification to behaviour that in any other context would be questioned and challenged. Therefore, when like Rebekah we act in isolation from the community of wisdom, we justify our behaviour with the defence that "love is love"!

Take a moment to reflect on the following questions:

What is more important to you, how you feel or what is right?

Are you involved in any relationships or conversations where how you feel (negatively or positively) is prejudicing your responses or decisions?

Is there anything you are currently doing where the sole justification is based on how you feel? Is it time to think again or allow the community of wisdom to speak again?

Educated by what she experienced

"Abraham was now very old, and the Lord had blessed him in every way. He said to the chief servant in his household, the one in charge of all that he had, 'Put your hand under my thigh. I want you to swear by the Lord, the God of heaven and the God of earth, that you will not get a wife for my son from the daughters of the Canaanites, among whom I am living, but will go to my country and my own relatives and get a wife for my son Isaac.'" (Genesis 24:1-4)

Rebekah became the wife of Isaac because Abraham put a plan into play. He didn't want his son to marry a Canaanite woman, so he sent his servant to a context familiar to him, and to a family he could trust.[4] There is no hint in the text that Abraham's actions were motivated by a word from God, but the urgency seemed to come from the fact that he was old and wanted Isaac married before he died. Though the hand of the Lord was clearly at work in guiding

---

4. Rebekah was the granddaughter of Nahor and Milcah and Nahor was Abraham's brother. Genesis 24:15.

Abraham's servant, who asked the Lord for His help, the plan that took Rebekah from Paddan Aram to the land of promise was both simple and meticulous.

As we observe Rebekah's plan in chapter twenty-seven, every detail is covered and nothing is left to chance. Just like the plan that brought her to Isaac, it is simple in nature and meticulous in its execution. Look at the clues in the chapter:

"Now Rebekah was listening as Isaac spoke to his son Esau." (27:5)

"When Rebekah was told what her older son Esau had said..." (27:42)[5]

"Now, my son, listen carefully to what I tell you." (27:8)

"My son, let the curse fall on me. Just do what I say, go and get them for me." (27:13)

"...so I can prepare some tasty food for your father, just the way he likes it." (27:9)

"...she prepared some tasty food, just the way his father liked it." (27:14)

"Then Rebekah took the best clothes of Esau... and put them on... Jacob." (27:15)

"She also covered his hands and the smooth part of his neck with the goatskins." (27:16)

"Flee at once to my brother Laban in Haran." (27:43)

"I'm disgusted with living because of these Hittite women. If Jacob takes a wife from among the women of this land, from Hittite women like these, my life will not be worth living." (27:46)[6]

---

5. Coincidence or had Rebekah got her "feelers" out?

6. This would have resonated with Isaac's experience (via Abraham's motivation) and also touched a nerve due to the grief he felt over Esau's Hittite wives. By sending Jacob back to Paddan Aram, Rebekah reverted to what she knew had worked and would work.

In the brilliance of her plan only one thing is missing. Nowhere does Rebekah enquire of the Lord. Nowhere does she pause to ask if her plan is His plan, or if He has a better way.

Why didn't she ask?

Maybe she didn't ask because the urgency of the moment demanded immediate action. Maybe she was so convinced she was right – that the older will serve the younger – that she didn't feel the need to ask. Or maybe she didn't ask because she didn't want to know!

Rebekah had witnessed the power of a plan in her own life, so when the moment arose to push her son before the face of her aging husband, she had a plan and executed it flawlessly.

One of the great tensions we must be aware of and learn to manage is that between our intellect and God's wisdom. Solomon urges us,

"Trust in the Lord with all your heart and lean not on your own understanding…" (Proverbs 3:4-5)

But he also warns (twice),

"There is a way that seems right to a man, but in the end it leads to death." (Proverbs 14:12 and 16:25)

This is the challenge. From my journey, experience and study of the Scriptures I know for absolute certainty that God's ways are better than mine. His wisdom is smarter than mine and His plan is greater than mine, yet there have been (and still are) moments when my way seems right to me. Rebekah's plan seemed right to her (hence she didn't ask the Lord for His advice) and some will argue her plan was right. But when we pursue a course of action that seems right to us, without consulting the wisdom of the Lord, we open ourselves up to the possibility that the plan that looked good can be anything but good. We must never only ask "Is this a good thing?". We must go further and ask, "Is this a God thing?" There will be moments when our good thing is in fact a God thing, but we must not fall into the temptation of equating our presumption with the Lord's purpose.

Take a moment to reflect on the following questions:

What plans are you pursuing at the moment? To what extent have you submitted or even surrendered them to the Lord?

Think of the people you influence. To what extent is your passion driving their purpose?

If Rebekah was shaped by what she heard, impacted by what she saw, motivated by what she felt, and educated by what she experienced, then it is not surprising that she did what she did in the way that she did it. Something was formed in her that was so powerful that she "fettered" her son to her plan and fractured her family in the process. Jacob found himself, for a few cataclysmic moments, a bit-player in another person's dream, convinced that this was for himself, when in fact it may have been for her. Rebekah's passion was admirable, and her ambition was undeniable, but the sheer force with which she drove the narrative swept the three men in her life along, whether it was the right thing or not. Rebekah won the day, but the question remains, was her dream the Lord's way?

Chapter Four – Esau: Assuming Another's Identity

Genesis 27:15-19

Jacob's story reached a dramatic tipping-point when the ambition of Rebekah combined with the compliance of her youngest son. Within the Torah it is summarised so simply but powerfully:

"Then Rebekah took the best clothes of her older son, which she had in the house, and put them on her younger son Jacob." (Genesis 27:15)

As if to drive the point home, we have this repeated idea in the very next verse:

"She also covered his hands and the smooth part of his neck with the goatskins."

The connection between verses 15 and 16 is softened a little in the NIV, which translates *lābaš* as "covered", when it might be better rendered "put on". Rebekah *put* Esau's clothes on Jacob and *put* the skins on his body. By implication, Jacob willingly received and participated in the transaction. The moment Jacob accepted what had been *put on* him, he assumed the identity of another and found himself playing a part for which he was never designed nor destined. The actions that followed therefore were simply the natural outcome of accepting another man's clothes.

Why would Jacob accept his brother's clothes? Why would he allow animal skins to be strapped to his body? Why did he buy into a process that was so obviously flawed?

As Jacob tried to get comfortable in clothes not designed for him, he ignored or failed to grasp a relentless truth when it comes to our God-shaped identity and our God-designed destiny:

"If we have to wear a disguise to get what we want, then what we want is not ours to have!"

And yet, the youngest son of Isaac, the favoured son of Rebekah, accepted the disguise that was *put on* him. But why?

To Hide (who he was)

The dictionary defines a disguise as "a means of altering one's appearance to conceal one's identity". Because of Isaac's love for Esau, Jacob knew he was not enough for this moment – that if he entered his father' presence as himself he would be rejected or possibly cursed. In order to draw near to his father, Jacob felt compelled to hide himself and cover up who he truly was.

This cover-up is an echo of an earlier episode in the Torah, when the first man and woman sinned in the garden of Delight. When their eyes are opened their reaction is twofold:

"... so they sewed fig leaves together and made coverings for themselves."

"... and they hid from the Lord God among the trees of the garden." (Genesis 3:7-8)

It is easy to miss the detail here, but we notice that they "sewed fig leaves" as "coverings". In other words, they took a material never intended for the purpose for which it was used, to cover up something that was always intended to be naked. The fig leaves became the first disguise of humanity, used to alter the man and woman's appearance to conceal their identity. The word used for covering ḥªgôrāh, is fascinating as it points not to clothing, but some form of sash or belt covering the loins. Essentially, the genitalia of our first parents were covered by the leaves, thus disguising their unique, God-shaped image, altering their appearance and concealing their true identity. When they subsequently hid themselves from the Lord God, this was the inevitable external consequence of an internal philosophical shift. No longer were they "naked without shame", living in the freedom of their God-given authenticity, they were now covered in their new disguise and thus experienced for the first time the burden of pretence and the power of the separation it produced.

Jacob followed the exact same pattern. His "fig leaves" were his brother's clothes and goatskins, and he used them to cover his true identity in the hope that he could fool the man who gave him life.

There is another remarkable connecting coincidence between these two stories. When the Lord is confronted with Adam and Eve's behaviour in the garden, He responds by asking three questions:

"Where are you?" (Genesis 3:9)

"Who told you that you were naked?"

"Have you eaten from the tree from which I have commanded you not to eat?" (Genesis 3:11)

If the Lord knew the answer to all these questions (and as the All-Knowing God we know He did), then why did He ask them?

I believe His questions were not an attempt to glean information, but rather an opportunity for the couple to move into the freedom of truth. If they could step from behind the bushes and be honest with Him, then perhaps they could take off their disguises and be naked before Him.

As Jacob knelt before Isaac (we'll deal with this encounter in the next chapter), Isaac too asked three questions:

"Who is it?" (Genesis 27:18)

"How did you find it so quickly, my son?" (Genesis 27:20)

"Are you really my son Esau?" (Genesis 27:24)

Unlike the Lord God of the garden, Isaac did not know the answer to the questions before he asked them (although he may have had his doubts). Nevertheless, like the questions posed in the garden, they gave Jacob the opportunity to step away from the bushes of a dangerous agenda. Isaac's questions offered Jacob three redemptive moments to drop the disguise and step into the light as his naked self, face to face with his father.

Since the garden, humans have become experts at hiding their true *face* from the world we inhabit. Sometimes we do so because of the prospect of persecution or the pressure of our peers, but perhaps more subtly and destructively, because of how we see ourselves. We are trapped by a perspective of poverty that empowers the view that "I am not enough". Like our first parents, we cover our God-shaped image out of shame, ignorant of the glory of our nakedness. Or, like Jacob, we disguise who we are out of insecurity and inadequacy, convinced that that person is not enough. We accept what others, life, and even a distorted view of self has put on us, remaining in the disguise that "alters our appearance and conceals our identity". The tragedy is that even if we put on *Esau's clothes*, we are still *Jacob*. Even if our disguise is so good that it fools those closest to us, we still have to live with the person we truly are.

Remember:

> **"You will never have to wear a disguise**
> **to get what the Lord has for you."**

To Become (who he was not)

"I am Esau your firstborn." (Genesis 27:19)

Not only did Jacob take Esau's clothes, but to see the deception through, he had to take Esau's name. Note his nervousness in the text. Jacob says, "your firstborn", as if Isaac didn't know that! If we have followed the pattern of the story so far, this moment, though sad and even shocking should not surprise us. We have seen Jacob *wrestle* with his brother in the womb, *grasp* his brother's heel, *buy* his birthright, and now he is on the verge of *stealing* the blessing due to Esau.

Jacob entered a room and committed one of the most audacious acts of deception in the whole of the Torah, and to succeed he had to become someone he was not. As Sacks concludes: "One thing stands out about the first phase in Jacob's life. He longs to be Esau – more specifically, he desires to occupy Esau's place... Why? The answer seems clear. Esau is everything Jacob is not. He is the firstborn."[1]

Note that thought: "Esau is everything Jacob is not." When Jacob put on his brother's clothes he was only hiding, because he was still himself in different clothes. But when he took his brother's name, he went from hiding who he was to pretending to be someone else. When he said, "I am Esau..." he stole his brother's identity and became, if only for a few nervous moments, a different person!

When I was a child one of the programmes I loved to watch was *Mr Benn*. Even though the format of the program was essentially the same for every episode, I could not wait for the following instalment because I wondered who Mr Benn would become next. On the surface of it, Mr Benn was an ordinary man, who lived in an ordinary house (52 Festive Road, London) and had an ordinary life, dressed in his black suit and black bowler hat. But Mr Benn had an incredible secret life. He would visit a fancy-dress costume shop, where he was given a costume to try on. Instead of leaving through the front door, Mr Benn went through a magic door at the back of the changing room and entered a world that was connected to his costume. When his adventure was over, the shopkeeper always

---

1. Rabbi Jonathan Sacks, *Covenant & Conversation: Genesis*, p.225.

appeared, ready to lead him back to the shop, where he would change his clothes and return to his normal life. What an exciting idea, that with a little imagination Mr Benn could become anyone he wanted to be. However, as each episode ended, it reminded us that he *had* to return to his reality – to be the man he really was and leave behind the man he was pretending to be.

It is one thing to wear a disguise to conceal who we are, but another to step into a different identity. When I wear a disguise I hide myself, but when I embrace pretence, I become someone else. Though these ideas are closely related, they require a shift in mindset and different skills. One of my favourite hobbies is to watch good movies and it never ceases to amaze me how an actor can become someone else for the sake of a script, and perform that role so well that I am completely convinced that what I saw was real. In 2020 at the 92nd Academy Awards, Joaquin Phoenix received an Oscar for best actor, awarded for his portrayal of the Joker, Batman's nemesis. In the movie that charted the emergence and development of the Joker, Phoenix's acting was gloriously disturbing, presenting a version of his character that most had never seen, while at the same time making sense of why the Joker was the way he was. The audience was drawn in because he had completely immersed himself in his character. We believed because he *became*!

To pretend is to "make it appear that something is the case when in fact it is not". This was what Mr Benn did every episode and what Joaquin Phoenix did in *The Joker*. But at least we knew they were just pretending. When Jacob said, "I am Esau", only Rebekah knew that he was pretending; Isaac believed he was who he said he was. Jacob pretended to be someone else with the express purpose of misleading his father and manipulating his circumstances. Hiding can be relatively easy, for all we need is a disguise and, if needed, a place to run. But pretending to be someone we are not requires a much greater level of commitment. To hide, Jacob only had to put something on, but to pretend he had to *become*. To hide, no words were required, but to pretend, he had to learn a script and stick to it, even when his father tested it with his questions. To hide, he could stand alone in his brother's clothes, but to pretend he had to move beyond self, isolation and comfort and face a world where others would be impacted by what he was and wasn't. To hide, Jacob had little to do (and what he did do was relatively easy), but to pretend required unwavering commitment and relentless energy. Hiding may be easy but pretending is exhausting.

Remember:

"You will never have to pretend to be someone else to get what the Lord has for you."

To Get (what was not his)

There is a possible interesting word connection between the actions of Rebekah, Jacob, and what the Law would later forbid.

"Then Rebekah took the best clothes of Esau her older son..." (Genesis 27:15)

One translation translates "best" as "choicest" garments,[2] as the word used (*ḥᵃmŭḏôṯ*), points to something that is considered valuable and the best. The root of this word is *ḥāmaḏ*, which expressed as a verb means "to take pleasure in, to desire, lust after or covet". It is this word that we see used in the tenth Commandment:

"And you shall not *covet* your neighbour's house. You shall not *covet* your neighbour's wife... or anything that belongs to your neighbour." (Exodus 20:17)[3]

---

2. JPS, 1917
3. My italics added

Jacob in effect puts on the best (*ḥāmad*) robe Esau has, because he desires (*ḥāmad*) what rightfully belongs to his brother. His actions are not motived by destiny but desire, not by glory but by greed, and not for purpose, but his own position. Jacob's actions are the embodiment of that forbidden later in the Law, namely, to desire what another has and seek to take it from him.

Another interesting reflection is the symmetry of the Ten Commandments. The first four words/Commandments speak to our relationship with the Lord and finish with commandment number four:

"Remember the Sabbath day by keeping it holy..." (Exodus 20:8)

This is the longest commandment of the Ten.

The last six words/Commandments speak to our relationship with people and finish with commandment number ten:

"And you shall not covet..." (Exodus 20:17)

This is the only command with a double emphasis, repeating the word covet twice. So we see that the final God-focused Commandment is the longest and has "rest" at its heart, centred on our relationship with the Lord. The final human-focused Commandment (the only one with a repeat idea) places the welfare of our neighbour before self, cautioning us against the desire to possess the world they inhabit. Could it be that if we live at rest, enter into Sabbath, and walk in the security of the knowledge that we are loved, valued and provided for, that the need to become someone else and to take what they have will be eradicated?

Whether this is an idea worthy of consideration or not, in Jacob we observe a young man not at rest with his God and not at ease with himself – all of which adds to the impulse to hide who he was, to be who he was not, in order to get what ultimately was not his. Jacob wanted the blessing, and who doesn't want to be blessed, but this particular blessing was not his to take and never his to have.

However, his coveting desire drove him to do what he probably never imagined he would do.

Jacob succeeded in stealing what was not his, but even here the story has an interesting twist which speaks to this moment. When Isaac gave the *first blessing* to Jacob, he thought he was giving it to Esau, but later, when the act of deceit came to light and Jacob was forced to leave, Isaac gave a *second blessing* to Jacob... this time knowing who was before him:

"May God Almighty bless you and make you fruitful and increase your numbers until you become a community of peoples. May He give you and your descendants the blessing given to Abraham, so that you may take possession of the land where you now live as an alien, the land God gave to Abraham." (Genesis 28:3-4)

This blessing not only connects Jacob back to Abraham but is incredibly similar to that given to Isaac himself by the Lord (Genesis 26:2-5) – a blessing that relates to a promise that speaks of both people and land.

Was this *second blessing* Jacob received really the first one he would have received had he not panicked and took matters into his own hands?

Is the Lord showing Jacob that if he will rest in His promise, that everything he is supposed to have he will get, and all without disguise or pretence?

Had Jacob waited, would he have got this blessing anyway?

I know these questions are all matters for conjecture, but the blessing Isaac gave when he thought Jacob was Esau is significantly different to the one he gave when he knew Jacob was Jacob. Presented with disguise and pretence, Isaac gave the right thing to the wrong person, but then presented with truth, *face to face* with his youngest son, Isaac gave to Jacob what was his in the first place.

What a lesson the Torah begs us to learn. To get what the Lord has promised we don't have to wear a disguise and hide ourselves. We don't have to pretend to be someone else, and we don't have to manipulate, jockey, pull, push or cheat. We are called to rest in the One who promised and trust in His ability to get us where we need to go. I love how Proverbs puts it:

"The king's heart is in the hand of the Lord; He directs it like a watercourse wherever He pleases." (Proverbs 21:1)

We must trust in the One who has us in His hand and rest in His ability to give to us whatever we need in order to do whatever He wants us to do. When we are in His rest then we won't want or need what "Esau" is or has, because we trust the One who knows our name, sets our course and has our best interests at heart.

Do you trust His promise?

Can you trust His power?

Are you willing to trust His process?

If we are humble enough to believe that whatever blessing awaits, the Lord of blessing will give it to us, then we are less likely to put on a disguise and hide our true self, and more likely to resist the call of pretence.

Remember:

"You will never have to break His rules to get what the Lord has for you."

Take a moment to reflect on the following questions:

Why do you cover up?

Have you accepted another's clothes, put on you by someone else?

Are you striving to make God's promise happen in your own strength or are you trusting He can make it happen?

Chapter Five – Isaac: Abusing Another's Trust

Genesis 27:18-29

The moment Jacob uttered the words, "My father," he reached the point of no return. As he approached Isaac, there was still a chance that his mission could be aborted, but as his words broke the silence, so began one of the most calculated and callous episodes of deception in the whole of the Torah. Jacob, who would in the future rise to be one of the greatest Patriarchs in biblical history, entered his father's presence as a common thief, pushed on by the ambition of his mother and hidden in the clothes of his brother.

It was one thing to pretend in private, with only his mother as an audience, but as he stood before Isaac, his private pretence became a public masquerade, and everything was on the line. Jacob had demonstrated guile and business savvy when he *bought* his brother's birthright. No deceit was required when negotiating with Esau, only the ability to manipulate and take advantage of his brother's immaturity and stupidity. But now, to steal Esau's blessing, Jacob had to move from negotiation to seduction, and from business savvy to a dangerous game of bluff.

Jacob's skill in pretence is highlighted through two key statements in the text. As Isaac examined Jacob, it says:

"He did not recognise him..." (Genesis 27:23)

The word translated "recognise" is *nāḵar* and is used here in a way that shows Isaac investigated his son, in order to know or confirm something. So convincing was Jacob's performance and his disguise, that Isaac later concluded to Esau:

"Your brother came deceitfully and took away your blessing." (Genesis 27:35)

Some Bible versions translate "deceitfully" as "guile" or "subtlety", because the word *mirmāh* points to the idea of intentionally misleading someone by distorting or holding back the truth.

There is a fascinating use of the word *nākar* later in the Torah in the story of Joseph:

"As soon as Joseph saw his brothers, he recognised them (*nākar*), but he pretended (*nākar*) to be a stranger and spoke harshly to them. 'Where do you come from?' he asked.

'From the land of Canaan,' they replied, 'to buy food.'

Although Joseph recognised (*nākar*) his brothers, they did not recognise (*nākar*) him." (Genesis 42:7-8)

Why did they not recognise him? Because he was disguised, hidden, and in a form that they neither remembered nor understood. They weren't looking for Joseph in Egypt, so they simply didn't see him. Unlike Jacob, Joseph did not deliberately disguise himself in order to deceive his brothers, but once he recognised them, he did nothing to help them see who he was. He ensured they did not recognise him until he was ready to be seen.

Jacob hid himself well and played the role of his brother brilliantly and boldly, because he knew at some point his disguise would be investigated and his pretence tested. Unlike Esau, Isaac was neither immature nor foolish, and Jacob understood that his father's senses, heightened by the demise of his sight, would be on high alert, probing for all that was not true. To fool Isaac, Jacob had to pull off the performance of a lifetime, not merely by playing the part, but by becoming the person.

If Jacob could dupe his father, how easy is it for us to hide ourselves, wear a disguise and fool the world around us in the process? Deception is not difficult for most humans to do, but it is exhausting to maintain. The effort and energy required in developing a new wardrobe, applying make-up and learning the ways of another is colossal, as is both the skill and stealth required in maintaining such a rouse in front of those closest to us. Jacob demonstrates that the Isaacs' in our world can be fooled, misled and duped, but at what cost? When we choose pretence over authenticity and disguise over reality, two great bedrock ideas will always be sacrificed on the altar of expediency: namely **truth** and **trust**. We must ask ourselves the question: *Is anything worth such a cost?*

As Jacob engaged with his father, the Torah shows us the consistent eradication of *truth* and the relentless erosion of *trust*. For Jacob, his brother's blessing was worth such a price and the greater gain was worth the moral pain. Later he would come to know the bankruptcy of his actions, but as he stood before his father he was sure that pretence was a necessary evil to achieve both his prosperity and purpose.

We must remember:

> **"If we have to deceive those around us to get what we want, then what we want is not ours to have!"**

The subtext of this particular episode is the vulnerability of the Patriarch. This is introduced to us at the beginning of chapter 27, when we are told:

"… Isaac was old and his eyes were so weak that he could no longer see…" (Genesis 27:1)

It was precisely because of this vulnerability that Isaac took the initiative to address the issue of *the blessing* and prepare his sons for the future. The word translated "weak" is *kāhāh* and points to the idea of something being so weak that it cannot function. In this context it seems that Isaac's eyes were dim and expressionless, thus leaving him reliant on the words and actions of those around him. Isaac's condition therefore created an opportunity for his sons to either cover his weakness with humble, honest, honourable service – affording both protection and strength to their father – or to take advantage of his weakness and exploit the man of God for their own agenda. Jacob chose the latter and the text shows us his brazen abandonment of the truth and his heartless destruction of trust, knowing that in order for his pretence to succeed, these two pillars of integrity had to be dismantled.

If we are to escape the tyranny of pretence and live in the freedom of authenticity, we must embrace the power of *truth* and *trust*. If we speak out of the truth of our God-shaped identity and remain faithful to it, through our actions and lifestyle, we will become a person and create a world that is truly trustworthy. The world we inhabit and the people closest to us may not be *blind,* like Isaac, but they are just as vulnerable to our sleight of hand and manipulation; to words that misdirect and actions that mislead. In my world, which includes my family, my local church, friends and a teaching ministry that takes me around the planet, I engage with people who are willing to believe the truth of my words and trust my actions. They want to believe that what they hear and see is genuine and that under the titles and the clothes and the ministry CV, I really am *Jacob* and not someone else in disguise! Rarely has my world demanded perfection from me, but it does deserve an "authentic me".

Let me reflect directly for a moment with leaders, shepherds, teachers and preachers. Through the breath-taking advance of technology, we live in a truly globalized world. From my smartphone I can potentially connect to anyone and anything, just about anywhere. Christians can listen to and watch their favourite preacher and teacher without leaving the comfort of their home, and today like never before the temptation of comparison and the tyranny of competition lurks beyond every click. We feel the pressure to make our "set" look like theirs, to have the cool clothes they are wearing and to find those killer one-liners that rock the audience (and maybe to even say them like they do!) Even if we don't fall into the trap of copying others, there's the pressure of borrowing their ideas without ever owning their journey.

I remember teaching in a context where I was asked during one service to address an audience populated almost entirely by young adults. As I entered the building ready to teach and with the word burning inside me, I was greeted with a statement that rocked me a little:

"I hope you're going to be young and trendy tonight!"

Now, I am a pretty secure human. I've been in full time Christian ministry since 1987 and I have a clear idea of who I am and who I'm not; of what I can do and what I can't. But that little statement got under my skin. As I took my place on the front row it gnawed away in my mind… "be young and trendy" …and as I worshipped it harassed me… *be young and trendy?* At the heart of my torment was not the statement itself but my ego. I wanted to be liked. I wanted to be trendy and I wanted the young adults to love me. Thus, for a few moments, I contended (at the age of 53) with the idea of abandoning me for the lure of another identity. Fortunately, I came to my senses, repented of my stupidity and had the confidence and courage to remain myself… but it was close!

I love how Solomon put it:

"A heart at peace gives life to the body, but envy rots the bones." (Proverbs 14:30)

Whatever we are saying, let it be truth-filled!

However we are behaving, let it be trust-worthy!
We must remember:

"If we have to deceive those around us to get what we want, then what we want is not ours to have!"

The Torah is relentless in casting its spotlight on the sacrifice of *truth* and *trust* throughout this story, highlighting Jacob's behaviour through three answers and three actions. Let's take a closer look.

Jacob's three answers – the eradication of Truth

Isaac asked three questions as Jacob approached him. In effect he gave Jacob three opportunities to tell the truth.

Question #1:
"Who is it?" (v18)

Jacob answered:
"I am Esau, your firstborn. I have done as you told me. Please sit up and eat some of my game so that you may give me your blessing." (v19)

Notice how Jacob quickly deflected the identity question/answer and turned it into an action that required a response from his father. He cleverly moved the focus of attention off himself and onto Isaac. Jacob knew that he could not hang around the identity issue too long or he would be found out, so he shifted the conversation onto what Isaac actually wanted.

   Over the years I've noticed that often when we ask, "Who are you?" or "Why don't you introduce yourself to us?", the answer is usually more about what the person does than who they are. As humans, we so easily slip into *actions* and *achievements* as an explanation of *identity*, rather than simply being able to answer, "I am..." *Who are you* is a relatively easy question to answer, yet its simplicity probes the heart of our self-image and our security within it. If I am at ease with who I am, then "I am John" will suffice, but if I am not at rest, or if the world that is asking is not content with such a simple, honest and forthright answer, then we find ourselves padding our *who* with *what*.

There is, of course, nothing wrong with talking about what we do, as long as it is not a deflection from who we are. Even in the Church we fall into this trap. Rarely is a leader, speaker or teacher introduced to a congregation or conference by their name alone. Usually we feel the pressure and expectation to explain what they have done and why that gives them the license and authority to stand before us. Don't get me wrong, there is nothing wrong with this and I appreciate why we do it (I have done it many times myself when introducing others), but by doing it, we subtly reinforce the idea of *what* rather than *who*. When speaking of what a person does, it must always be an affirmation of who they are, never a deflection from it.

Jacob's deflection tactic worked, at least initially, but perhaps sensing that something wasn't right, Isaac asked a second, more probing question.

Question #2:
"How did you find it so quickly, my son?" (v20)

Jacob answered:
"The Lord your God gave me success." (v20)

I suspect Jacob had not reckoned on his father going down this route and therefore he had not rehearsed a reasonable answer. So, when put on the spot, I suggest he panicked and reached for the *nuclear option*, playing the God-card to his father in the hope that this answer would end the investigation and move proceedings quickly to *the blessing*. Jacob appealed, not to *his* God, but the Lord of his father who had answered his prayer and blessed him and Rebekah in their barrenness[1]; who later appeared to him in Gerar and gave him a promise[2]; and to whom Isaac built an altar on receiving the assurance of His presence.[3] Up to this moment in the life of Jacob there is not a single reference to him engaging with the Lord in any way. In fact, it seems that the Lord is completely absent from Jacob's thinking, except in this self-serving moment. Isaac however, after the trauma of Moriah, had found the Lord for himself and was clearly not just in covenant with the Lord, but also evidently in communion with Him.

Jacob moved from deflection to desperation, using God as a bargaining tool in his pretence. In doing so he invented a whole new narrative with the "G word" at the centre of it. Unfortunately, I have seen this too many times within my service of the Church; scenarios where individuals, in order to get what they want, play the God card knowing that no other card in the pack can trump it. "God has told me... God spoke to me in a dream... I got a prophetic word that said... I believe God wants me to do this..." Do I believe that God speaks to us? Of course, and I continue to encourage that expectation. But I am also convinced that we should not use God's name to affirm an identity He did not create nor endorse an agenda He did not initiate. Eventually, what seems right to us will be found out, and in my experience the one name that suffers in such moments is not ours, but His! When Jacob uttered those treacherous words to his father, he not only shamed himself, he also defamed the name of the Lord. The Lord had nothing to do with this moment, having never

---

1. Genesis 25:21
2. Genesis 26:2-6
3. Genesis 26:23-25

been consulted by Jacob. If He had been asked, His answer would not have required Jacob to dress up as his brother!

Having heard the trump card played, Isaac returned to the question he started with, but now in a different and much more direct form.

Question #3:

"Are you really my son Esau?" (v24)

Some translations present this as,

"Art though my *very* son."[4]

This phrase "very son" was also used by Isaac in verse 21.

The double emphasis of this phrase by Isaac in these two verses show us the urgency of his quest and the seriousness of the question. He must know who is before him because of the immensity of what he is about to give away.

Jacob answered:

"I am." (v24)

Note the difference in the answer given here to that of verse 19. Previously he said, "I am Esau, your firstborn," but now he lets the words Isaac spoke frame his succinct response. With such a short answer Jacob was in fact saying, "I am the one you think I am. I am the one you hope I am."

Jacob moved from deflection to desperation and now to flat out deception. Isaac needed to know that the man in front of him was his *very son*, and Jacob's answer, cold and concise, was the final statement of deception. Jacob did nothing to dissuade his father from his growing conviction that the man in front of him was in fact Esau!

There is a type of deception that comes about when we set out to deceive people: we pretend to be what we are not and assume another

---

4. JPS and CWSB

identity to serve our purposes or protect ourselves. But there is another, perhaps more subtle form of deception, that happens within and around us. It is the deception that, when others see us in a certain way, or *want* to see us a certain way, rather than putting them straight and gently bringing them back to reality, we affirm their version of us by playing along. We like the version of us they have formed in their mind, no doubt encouraged by our own words and actions. With a narrative now taking shape, we need only occasionally nod in the right places while their imagination does the rest. This is the idea behind the phrase "playing to the gallery", for in so doing, we behave in a way that will make people admire or support us.[5] If this *play* requires some engineering of our image and identity, or even comes at the expense of what is truly important, it is a price worth paying for the applause of the crowd. How tempting it is to live with the illusion others have created of us, especially when it allows us to get what we want from them!

When people cannot see they rely on truth!

When we speak of who we are, others depend on the truth of our words. At times, if necessary, we may need to challenge their view of who they think we are. Those who cannot see below the surface are dependent on what we say of ourselves. Those who *think* they see us, or want to see us in a certain way, need our commitment to the truth of who we really are – even if that ultimately disappoints the gallery! Truth is always important, but when the "Isaacs" in our world can't see us for who we really are, or want to see us as someone else, truth sits at the heart of both our definition and destiny.

---

5. dictionary.cambridge.com

Jacob's three actions – the erosion of Trust

Not only did Isaac ask three questions, he also requested three things that required specific, intimate actions from Jacob. If the questions probed for truth, then these actions would help Isaac determine if what he heard could be reconciled to what he experienced and felt. All three requests of Isaac and actions of Jacob are linked by the same word – *nāgas̆* – as Isaac searched for the solid ground of trust. On each of the three occasions, he asked Jacob to step away from the protection of the right answer and, in trust, *come near* to him in a *face to face* encounter. For only in coming near can truth be tested and trust proved.

Request #1:

"*Come near (nāgas̆)* so I can touch you my son, to know whether you really are my very son Esau or not." (v21)

Note this request follows the audacious claim of Jacob that the Lord had given him success. Isaac now tests the veracity of these words by an action that will require coming so close that he can *feel* his son.

Jacob's action:

"So Jacob *went close (nāgas̆)* to his father Isaac, who touched him…" (v22)

Ironically, this was the very thing Jacob feared the most when he protested to Rebekah:

"What if my father touches me?" (v12)

The word translated "touches" (in verse 12 and "touched" in v22) is *māsas̆* which carries the thought of touching and feeling something or someone with a view to identifying or understanding that thing or person. Thus, it fits with an idea we've already visited earlier in this chapter, when we noted that Isaac did not *recognise* him (v23).

The request that Jacob feared the most was the very thing Isaac demanded. It is one thing to deceive a person with our words, for that can happen from a distance, but to deceive someone when they feel or touch us requires another level of commitment. As Isaac's trembling hands reached out and groped for the arms of his son, Jacob had to hope that the animal skins would do their work. But what must have been going through the mind of Jacob as he watched his blind father search for truth through the touch of his fingers? Did he look at his father's expressionless eyes, searching in vain for confirmation of what his hands felt? Or did he look away, unable to *face* the depth of his own deception?

At this stage, Isaac still cannot square the circle of his own confusion, for he concludes:

"The voice is the voice of Jacob, but the hands are the hands of Esau." (v22)

In an attempt to reconcile this tension Isaac asked the third question.

Having been unconvinced by the first two answers of his son, Isaac hoped that the intimacy of touch would settle his nerves, but still unconvinced, he returned to the quest for truth. With the bold affirmation of Jacob in response to the third question, Isaac returned once more to the call of intimacy in a final attempt to settle the storm of doubt that raged within him.

Request #2:
"My son, *bring* me (*nāgas*) some of your game to eat..." (v25)

Another way of translating that verse could be:

"... bring it near to me..."

Jacob's action:
"Jacob *brought it* to him (*nāgas*) and he ate..." (v25)

Having *felt* his son, Isaac now eats with him in an act of communion. The sharing of food was the sharing of life and in the cultural context of their world, this was not just food and wine, this was the sharing of heart and self. Isaac reckoned that if this man was an imposter, the call to communion and the intimacy of the table would further probe for the chinks in the armour of his pretence. If the man before him was who he said he was, then the table would call him forth.

If we follow the text literally, no words were spoken between the two men as the game and wine were consumed, and we're not even certain how long the meal lasted. If there were words spoken no detail is given, but if no words were spoken and silence hung over the table, then that might explain Isaac's third and final request. Through his touch, he had felt his son and through his taste he had enjoyed the meal (after all, Rebekah had prepared it just the way Isaac liked it (Genesis 27:14). Now for the ultimate test...

Request #3:
"*Come here (nāgas)*, my son, and kiss me." (v26)

Jacob's action:
"So he *went to him (nāgas)* and kissed him..." (v27)

In the first request Jacob offered his hands to his father and through the second he brought him his food. But in the third request, he was being asked to offer himself to his father. This action brought him so close that nothing was between his father's face and his, so close that Isaac was able smell him.

What was Jacob thinking in that moment, when their two faces came together?

If Isaac could smell Jacob, then the opposite was true, and if Isaac kissed his son, then for the ruse to work, Jacob also had to kiss his father.

In this moment of apparent intimacy, Jacob betrays his brother, deceives his father and shames himself. This act of intimacy would forever live in infamy.

When we do not know we rely on trust

Over the years I have sat with people who have become aware that someone close to them, who they trusted, was not who they thought they were. A secret life is exposed, or unusual behaviour brought to light. On so many of those occasions it was clear that the person had no idea that the one they trusted was like this. Not only had they been deceived by words and lies, they had also been misled by actions. Actions that were so convincing in the context of intimacy, partnership and friendship, that they were genuinely shocked by what stood before them. It might be a leader with a double life; a husband with a pornographic mistress; a family member drowning in debt through gambling and greed; or a confidante who turned out to be a conspirator!

Through this episode in the life of Jacob and similar experiences, I am reminded of an enduring truth: that every action is a trust transaction. That through our actions we are either building trust or breaking it. If trust were a bank account, then our actions are either making deposits or withdrawals. Too many withdrawals will eventually leave us bankrupt and unable to trade.

When we fall into the trap of accepting another's dream and assuming another's identity, the inevitable consequence will be that of abusing another's trust. Truth and trust will be the primary casualties of such decisions, but the collateral damage will touch a world far beyond the epicentre of our choices. Therefore, as we journey in life we must remember:

"If we have to deceive those around us to get what we want, then what we want is not ours to have!"

The tyranny of pretence is both expensive and exhausting. Yet, frustratingly, it will *never* give us what we actually seek. No matter how good you are at being *Esau*, you will always be *Jacob*!

Take a moment to reflect on the following questions:

When asked who you are, how often do you embellish the answer with what you do?

Have you ever used God to serve your own agenda (when you knew deep down that He wasn't involved)? Why did you do this and how did it end?

Is there an Isaac in your world that you betrayed with your pretence? Is it possible to ask for forgiveness from them and/or make restitution to them?

Chapter 6 – Paying the Price

Genesis 27:30-28:9

Sir Isaac Newton's third law of motion states, "For every action, there is an equal and opposite reaction". In essence he discovered that in the physical world forces are the product of interactions, whether they are caused by direct contact or from a distance. Newton discovered that when I sit on my chair, not only is my body exerting a downward force on the chair, but my chair (and some chairs are better than others), is exerting an upward force on my body. The force from my body is often referred to as *action*, while the force from the chair to my body is called *reaction*. Forces, according to this law, always come in pairs!

Though Newton's law of motion applies primarily to our understanding of the physical world, it doesn't require much imagination to hear the echo of this law in Jacob's story. No sooner had Jacob left Isaac's presence with the prize of the *blessing*, than a series of reactions were set in motion which produced sad, even tragic consequences. The *force* exerted through Jacob's audacity can be clearly understood and measured by the *force* of the reactions that split this family for years to come. As Jacob was about to discover, pretence carried a heavy price tag, not just for him, but for everyone touched by it. The Torah doesn't hide the impact of his actions and the cost for all involved. Everyone paid something for Jacob's pretence.

Esau's distress

This is captured in a single statement in the text:

"Then Esau wept aloud." (Genesis 27:38)

The bitterness of this moment was expressed through the intensity of Esau's mourning, bringing to the surface previous resentment that had been buried and lay dormant.

"Isn't he rightly named Jacob? This is the second time he has taken advantage of me: He took my birthright, and now he's taken my blessing!" (Genesis 27:36)

Two things are worthy of note in this statement.

First, the play on Jacob's name. "This is the second time he has taken advantage of me…" The word translated here as "taken advantage" is *'āqab,* derived from the noun *'āqeb* which means "heel". It points to the idea of "grasping at the heel, supplanting or deceiving" – the very picture at the heart of Jacob's own name *ya'aqob.*[1] Esau lamented the fact that Jacob was *born grasping* and he was *still grasping.*

Second, notice how Esau interprets past events, showing himself to be the victim of Jacob's scheming, not once, but twice:

"He took my birthright… he's taken my blessing."

Esau places the loss of his birthright in the same category as that of the blessing, complaining that Jacob *took* them both; by implication, that he *stole* both. But the record shows that although Jacob used guile and skill in manipulating his brother, he did not *take* the birthright. Rather, Esau foolishly and flippantly sold it, concluding:

"What good is the birthright to me?"

The Torah adds the commentary:

"So Esau despised his birthright…" (Genesis 25:32 and 34)

Although at the time Esau didn't seem to care about his birthright, clearly he had come to regret his stupidity in selling something so precious so cheaply. Jacob bought the birthright and now, as distress

---

1. Genesis 25:26

and bitterness takes hold of Esau, he reinterprets the past. In his mind, at least, Jacob had stolen it!

When Esau realised that there was no blessing for him, and what Jacob had done could not be undone, his distress turned to anger and the focus of that anger was the eventual destruction of his brother:

"Esau held a grudge against Jacob because of the blessing his father had given him. He said to himself, 'The days of mourning for my father are near; then I will kill my brother Jacob.' (Genesis 27:41)

Some Bible versions translate this as, "Esau hated Jacob…" but what is certain is that unlike his previous resentment over the birthright, which remained under wraps until this moment, Esau did not hide his feelings nor his intentions concerning the blessing. Jacob would pay, and he would pay with his life.

Rebekah's deceit

As events started to take on a life of their own, Rebekah was forced to react in order to save both her sons and some semblance of normality within her family. Her desperation is summed up in her conclusion:

"Why should I lose both of you in one day?" (Genesis 27:45)

The word translated "lose" is *šāḵōl*, and points specifically to the idea of being deprived of children; therefore, by implication, of being left bereft. The weight of Rebekah's words point to the seriousness of the moment. She is now contending with a force of reaction from Esau that even she did not anticipate. She did not consult or involve Isaac in her new plan, but simply concluded that in order to save both her sons, one of them had to go!

Note how she arranged the exit plan:

"Then Rebekah said to Isaac, 'I'm disgusted with living because of these Hittite women. If Jacob takes a wife from among the women of this land, from Hittite women like these, my life will not be worth living.'" (Genesis 27:46)

Though Rebekah was not lying to Isaac, she was being deliberately deceitful in order to manipulate her husband into making the decision she needed him to make – without him knowing the true reason why he made it. Her statement had historic context to it, because we are told previously:

"When Esau was forty years old, he married Judith daughter of Beeri the Hittite, and also Basemath daughter of Elon the Hittite. They were a source of grief to Isaac and Rebekah." (Genesis 26:34-35)

This explains Isaac's immediate reaction in both blessing Jacob and sending him away.

"Then Isaac sent Jacob on his way…" (Genesis 28:5).

Sadly, Isaac thought he was sending Jacob away to protect him from those Hittite women he and Rebekah despised so much, but instead, he was sending him away from his brother, without ever confronting the issues at the heart of the grudge between them, and thus consigning them to years of unnecessary, painful separation. If the real reason for Jacob's departure came to light, Rebekah might have saved her sons, but may yet lose her husband.

Isaac's disappointment

This is not explicit in the text, but is implied ironically by Esau's actions once Jacob had departed.

"Now Esau learned that Isaac had blessed Jacob and had sent him to Paddan Aram to take a wife from there, and that when he blessed him he commanded him, 'Do not marry a Canaanite woman,' and that Jacob had obeyed his father and mother and had gone to Paddan Aram. Esau then realized how displeasing the Canaanite women were to his father Isaac; so he went to Ishmael and married Mahalath, the sister of Nebaioth and daughter of Ishmael son of Abraham, in addition to the wives he already had." (Genesis 28:6-9)

The Torah is never random, and what seems like an incidental inclusion about Esau's third wife may in fact be highlighting something of the pain and disappointment felt by Isaac over the whole affair. As we've seen previously in this chapter, Rebekah used Esau's Hittite wives to her advantage, for they were a "source of grief" to both her and Isaac. Could it be that in attempting to ease Isaac's pain, Esau married a relative of his father's half-brother? Was Esau so aware of his father's disappointment that he was prepared to go to extreme measures to help heal his wounds and ease his grief?

We are given no detail of Isaac's feelings and though I must be careful not to read anything into the text that is not there, I can only imagine the potential brokenness he felt, having been lied to so blatantly by one son, while trying to comfort his other son through the loss of his blessing. What had started so promisingly for Isaac that day had ended in sadness, disappointment and separation. When the dust of that day settled, his family would never be the same again.

Jacob's diversion

When Rebekah suggested to Jacob that he should leave home to go to her brother's house in Harran, it is clear that she was thinking short-term:

"Now then, my son, do what I say: Flee at once to my brother Laban in Harran. Stay with him for a while until your brother's fury subsides. When your brother is no longer angry with you and forgets what you did to him, I'll send word for you to come back from there." (Genesis 27:43-45)

Note the language:

"…until your brother's fury subsides…"

"When your brother is no longer angry with you…"

"…I'll send word for you to come back from there."

Knowing Esau, Rebekah was sure that his anger would blow over, that her beloved son would be able to return, and they would all live happily ever after. However, what started out as a temporary stop-gap, became a significant and lengthy division and tragically, for Rebekah, she never saw her son Jacob again. In fact, the potential chronology around Jacob's departure and eventual return is staggering.

We know he returned to the land of promise when he was around 97 years old,[2] and the oldest he could have been when he left his home is 63.[3] Some have suggested that Jacob was around 57 when he left the land of promise,[4] meaning that from his departure from home to his return to the land, there is a gap of between 34-40 years, depending on how we count. One further number worthy of our consideration is Isaac's age when he died. We know from the text that he was 180 years old. The Torah concludes:

"Jacob came home to his father Isaac in Mamre, near Kiriath Arba (that is, Hebron), where Abraham and Isaac had stayed. Isaac lived a hundred and eighty years. Then he breathed his last and died and was gathered to his people, old and full of years. And his sons Esau and Jacob buried him." (Genesis 35:27-29)

This text seems to imply that though Jacob returned to the land and, as we shall see later in this book, reconciled with Esau, he may

2. When Jacob joined Joseph in Egypt he was 130 and Joseph was 39. Therefore, Jacob was 91 when Joseph was born. After Joseph's birth Jacob wanted to return to the land (Gen. 30:25), but he stayed another 6 years and worked (Gen.31:41), then returned, thus making him 97.
3. Esau went to Ishmael to marry Mahalath and we know Ishmael died at 137 (Gen.25:17) and that he was 14 years older than Isaac (Abraham being 86 when Ishmael was born and 100 when Isaac was born (Gen.16:16 and 21:5)). So, the oldest Isaac could have been was 123, and Jacob was born when Isaac was 60 (Gen.25:26). Some timelines have him leaving aged 77, to fit with 20 years spent with Laban.
4. This would work if Jacob worked for Laban for 20 years then spent another 20 years, thus two lots of 20. When speaking to Laban he only references one period of 20 years that worked for him, because that was directly relevant in the conversation (Gen. 31:38-42).

not have returned directly or immediately to Isaac's house until his father's death. There is no mention of Rebekah, so we assume she died some time previous to this. If this is true, then when Jacob returned to the land, Isaac was between 157 and 163 years old, and if Jacob did not return to Isaac until the time of his death, then the *temporary separation* from home that Rebekah planned for Jacob had lasted between 57 and 63 years![5]

I wonder, if Jacob had known in advance the cost of his actions, would he have pursued the blessing so vigorously? Were there moments when he considered the fallout of that day and asked himself the question, *was it worth it?* These questions are, of course, pure conjecture, but the reactions to and consequences of Jacob's actions highlight for us a relentless tension in the biblical text when it comes to the life, identity and purpose of any individual.

Within the message of the Bible, we have the celebration of individuality but resistance to individualism. From the opening pages of Genesis, as we are led into the story of Creation, we see humans, male and female, made and shaped in the image of God, held up in their own right as a unique and special reflection of the Deity who made them. But no sooner do we see the glory of the individuals, than they are forged into a community; *one* person became *two* people and then the two became *one*! Framed in the creative order is the celebration of one, the individual, the man and the woman, and through them as individuals the making of a new and dynamic community. In many ways, how they are made and how they are called to behave is the very essence of the image of the God who created them. For when God said, "Let us make…" the individual genius of Father, Son and Spirit was seen to work in glorious synergy. Although the Bible highlights the work of each *Person* within the story, Creation is seen as the work of *all*.

---

5. If we accept Jacob was 20 years with Laban, then this means Jacob left at 77 and the time between Jacob leaving and Isaac's death is 43 years.

Individuality can be defined as "the quality or character of a particular person or thing that distinguishes them from others", whereas individualism is defined as "the habit or principle of being independent and self-reliant". One of the great dangers when engaging in conversation around our identity, is that our pursuit of individuality can quickly morph into an acceptance of individualism. Through individuality I celebrate who I am, but when I embrace individualism, then my individuality becomes my focus, my goal and my prize. Thus, being who I am or who I want to be is the most important thing, regardless of the impact this may have on the world I inhabit. This is not to contradict the trajectory of this book so far, but rather it is to interject a note of caution into our journey. The Bible is not a record of individuals, rather it's a record of community, into which individuals are called and through which they flourish. The God-community (Christians refer to this as the Trinity) calls out in the opening words of the text, and throughout the Scriptures God seeks to build a community in which His glory is made manifest and the diversity of our individuality is celebrated.

Born in the 1960s and raised and educated in the United Kingdom under the influence of Western philosophical rationale, I have observed that individualism has become a value of our civilisation. It is positioned as a freedom that others died to give us and therefore has become a right that we should possess, no matter what. In the West we celebrate not only our individuality but our right to both decide this and express it in whatever way we deem fit, regardless of context or community. For many Christians raised under this world-view, if we are not careful we fall into the temptation of reading the Bible through the lens of individualism. We are in danger of shaping the God at the heart of it into our image, as He becomes the God we want. If we are not careful, we learn to interpret the narrative of Scripture as a story that becomes about the individual alone. Subtly and dangerously, God becomes *mine* and His purpose is to do what *I want*. As we read the story, *me* replaces *we*, and *what I want* becomes more important than *what we need*.

Paul, writing to the called-out community at Ephesus concluded:

"For we are God's handiwork, created in Christ Jesus to do good works, which God prepared in advance for us to do." (Ephesians 2:10)

There is really only one way to read this: *we*. Yet, individualism – an understanding of individuality outside of community – will always subconsciously read this as *I*. Reading this verse as *I*, dramatically changes the focus and function of the text. Changing one word makes a story about *us* become all about *me*!

Let me illustrate through two very similar sounding statements, both written to the Church at Corinth. I've placed some insertions to help:

"Don't <u>you</u> (plural) know that <u>you</u> (plural) yourselves are God's <u>temple</u> (singular) and that God's Spirit dwells in your midst? If anyone destroys God's <u>temple</u> (singular), God will destroy that person; for God's <u>temple</u> (singular) is sacred, and <u>you</u> (plural) together are that <u>temple</u> (singular)." (1 Corinthians 3:16-17)

"Flee from sexual immorality. All other sins a person commits are outside the body, but whoever sins sexually, sins against their own body. Do <u>you</u> (plural) not know that your <u>bodies</u> (singular) are <u>temples</u> (singular) of the Holy Spirit, who is in you, whom <u>you</u> (plural) have received from God? <u>You</u> (plural) are not your own; <u>you</u> (plural) were bought at a price. Therefore honour God with your <u>bodies</u> (singular)." (1 Corinthians 6:18-20)

How powerfully the text changes and speaks when *I* is replaced with *we* and *you* doesn't always mean *me*.

In a culture where individuality has evolved into individualism, the Bible, my relationship with God, and my identity and purpose can all be subsumed into a world-view where I am at the centre, in which who I am and what I want is the most important thing. When this happens, the truth that we are individuals, fearfully and wonderful made, becomes the error of individualism; that I stand alone, I need no one else, and that the consequences of my decisions and actions don't matter. When it comes to living in the freedom of my God-shaped identity, the Bible is less concerned with my rights and more preoccupied with my responsibilities and how I use my freedoms. It is less indulgent when it comes to my individual wants and has more to say about the needs of the community I'm a part of.

I love how Paul positions this idea when trying to teach the outworking of this tension to the Church at Corinth. There was concern among the Christians around the issue of eating meat that had been offered to idols. Some didn't think it was right to do so while others thought it was fine. Paul's personal conclusion was that "…we are no worse off if we do not eat, and no better off if we do." (1 Corinthians 8:8). Therefore, as far as he was concerned, it was okay to do so.

However, he didn't leave the matter there, but offered an outstanding piece of wisdom, which not only helped the Corinthians but continues to help us when managing the tension of individuality and individualism and of the exercise of my rights and my responsibilities. Paul advised:

"Be careful, however, that the exercise of your rights does not become a stumbling block to the weak."

He reinforced this with his own personal commitment, concluding:

"Therefore, if what I eat causes my brother or sister to fall into sin, I will never eat meat again, so that I will not cause them to fall." (1 Corinthians 8:9 and 13)

Individualism says, "This is what I want and I don't care what you think, who it hurts or what impact it makes on my world." Paul understood that this mentality in his world would create only fracture, discord and pain. The pursuit of *I* alone, without considering the greater *we*, of which we are a part, will always lead to individualism being prized above community.

Our individuality is sacred, but individualism is to be resisted.

"Who I am" is vitally important, but never at the exclusion of where I am and how my preferences and choices impact my world.

When Jacob stood before his father, he was not thinking of the impact of his actions on Isaac, Rebekah or Esau. His focus was only on himself and how good the blessing would be for him. Ironically, as he chased the blessing, he surrendered his individuality – not in altruistic self-sacrifice for the betterment of others, but so that he could get what he wanted, concluding that the end justified the means. In order for Jacob to pull off this incredible act of deception his focus had to be entirely on himself, but the cost to his world in the pursuit of personal ambition through a disguised version of self would last for years to come. Later, much later, the Lord would make this individual a nation, but for now, sent from his home, Jacob lived for self and walked alone.

Take a moment to reflect on the following questions:

When you read the Bible do you tend to read it through the lens of I or we?

Next time you read a passage of Scripture, check out who the subject of the passage is, and if the "you" is singular or plural.

Is there any area of your life where healthy individuality has become dangerous or inward-looking individualism?

Chapter 7 – The Space In-Between

Genesis 28:10-31:55

Running away never solves anything, it merely transports the problem to another location. The years spent in Paddan Aram (however we count them), represented a formative liminal experience for Jacob. Having left the Land of Promise, he would one day return to fulfil a significant role, but for now, and for a while, he was confined to the *space in-between*. Rebekah had envisaged that her favoured son's time with her brother Laban would be a brief encounter, and we may assume that this was also in the back of Jacob's mind, but the Torah shows that the Lord had other plans.

Books could be written on Jacob's liminal season, for those years were packed with incident, intrigue, highs and lows, love, betrayal, prosperity and pain. Having left with only a staff, Jacob would eventually emerge from exile with two wives, eleven sons, one daughter and substantial wealth – all of which played its part in preparing him for an encounter with the face of God that would change him, and the nation within him, forever. Having disguised himself before the face of his father and run from the face of his brother, Jacob was about to see *The Face* that would forever change his face!

But before we get there (part 2 will explore in depth Jacob's *face to face* with God), let us consider briefly some significant moments in the space in-between that speak into and perhaps connect Jacob's two identity events. Jacob may have gone on the run, but the Lord was never off his case, and through the ups and downs in Paddan Aram, we observe the hand of the Lord nudging and guiding the process, desperate to get Jacob to a place of truth, authenticity and freedom.

I am glad that the Lord doesn't give up on the work of His hands too easily. Even when we are faithless, He remains faithful, and when we are determined to live our own way and do our own thing, because of His loving-kindness, He will do everything to win us back without violating or manipulating our freedom to choose. If we are to fulfil His greatest desire, to love Him "…with all our hearts, with all our souls and with all our strength…"[1] and thus bring Him delight, this must come from a heart that *wants to*, not one that *has to*.

The Lord loved and wanted Jacob, and had a plan for this stubborn grasper, but the glory and flaw at the heart of His plan is God's gift of freewill, which ensured He would not force Jacob to want Him. If the Lord was to become his God, and not just his father's, this had to come from his freewill and an authentic heart, because the Lord won't settle for anything less. Forced worship is an affront, while forced love is an insult to the Lord, and He wanted neither from Jacob.

If the space in-between teaches us anything, we learn that the Lord is patient with us and persistent in pursuing us. He does not want us to live under the tyranny of pretence nor the burden of someone else's purpose. He will do all He can to bring us to the freedom of our God-shaped identity and return us to the fulness of our God-designed destiny. But we must be willing to become and return!

A continuous factor at play in Jacob's in-between journey was his relationship with Laban. Having been sent from the presence of Isaac his father, Jacob found himself in the home and domain of his uncle Laban:

1. Deuteronomy 6:4-5

"Surely you are my bone and flesh." (Genesis 29:14)

Although welcomed with open arms, their somewhat adversarial and combative relationship formed a turbulent subtext to everything Jacob experienced there. Without knowing it, Laban became *the Lord's agent* in teaching Jacob lessons of the heart and life that he would never forget. Through Laban, the Lord nudged, prodded, challenged and provoked his runaway son, and though Jacob may not have appreciated it at the time, Laban's agenda would be used by the Lord to lead Jacob to freedom.

Laban Deceived him

Jacob's love for Rachel is arguably the most romantic story in the whole of the Torah. Three times in chapter 29 there is reference to his love for her:

"Jacob *loved* Rachel…" (v18)

"So Jacob served seven years for Rachel, and they seemed to him but a few days because of the *love* he had for her." (v20)

(Is that not one of the most romantic and beautiful things you've ever read?)

"…he *loved* Rachel more than Leah." (v30)[2]

This final reference in verse 30 introduces us nicely to the driver at the heart of Laban's deceit. Genesis 29:15-30 summarises for us Jacob's passionate desire for Rachel and his willingness to work seven years as payment for her, but we're also introduced to Laban's eldest daughter, Leah, who ended up becoming Jacob's first wife. Expecting to wake up with Rachel, Jacob woke up to find Leah in his bed and confronted Laban with a question so bursting with irony that it cannot be missed:

"Why have you deceived me?" (v25)

---

2. ESV

To ensure the irony is driven home, the Torah connects the two events by using the same word. The word used by Jacob here, *rāmāh*, is the same word used by Isaac when describing Jacob's behaviour to his brother Esau:

"Your brother came deceitfully (*mirmāh*) and he has taken away your blessing." (Genesis 27:35)

Jacob disguised himself to deceive Isaac and took what was not his, and now Leah is disguised and placed in Jacob's bed. This cannot be a coincidence. Rather, it points to a God-incidence, where Jacob experiences a taste of his own medicine and feels the pain, first-hand, of being duped and humiliated by someone he trusted.

Jacob in disguise had *deceived* Isaac, but through the disguise of another he was deceived.

Laban Defrauded him

"You know that I've worked for your father with all my strength, yet your father has cheated me by changing my wages ten times…" (Genesis 31:6-7)

Whatever else Jacob was, he was both intelligent and industrious. Having worked fourteen years for Laban's two daughters, he worked a further six years in Laban's house and it is clear that on numerous occasions Laban took advantage of him by adjusting his wages at least ten times in a six year period! Though Jacob confessed "God has not allowed him to harm me," the injustice clearly impacted him, eventually causing him to confront Laban about his behaviour (Genesis 31:41).

But again, through the genius of the Torah we hear another echo of what might be deemed fraudulent behaviour:

"First sell me your birthright." (Genesis 25:31)

As observed earlier in this book, Esau was both incredibly naïve and foolish to even consider selling his birthright, let alone for the bargain price of a bowl of his favourite stew. Some might conclude that Jacob did not break any laws in doing what he did, but he certainly violated the spirit of truth and decency in taking advantage of his brother, devaluing what was precious and defrauding someone he should have been protecting. Jacob, like Easu, carried the injustice; just as Jacob's pain was expressed to his wives and to Laban, so Esau's pain was expressed to his father Isaac:

"This is the second time he has taken advantage of me: He took my birthright, and now he's taken my blessing!" (Genesis 27:36)

Jacob *defrauded* his brother Esau, but through his uncle's behaviour he was also defrauded.

Laban wanted to Dominate him

Just after the birth of Joseph, Jacob had attempted to go back to the Land of Promise. Speaking to Laban he asked,

"Send me on my way so I can go back to my own homeland." (Genesis 30:25)

However, through a mixture of emotional coercion ("If I have found favour in your eyes please stay..." v27), spiritual manipulation, ("I have learned by divination that the Lord has blessed me because of you..." v27) and financial temptation, ("Name your wages, and I will pay them..." v28), Laban attempted once more to control and dominate his nephew. Jacob was right when he concluded that Laban had prospered because of his industry and the Lord's blessing (v's 29-30) and Laban knew it. Jacob was Laban's *golden goose*, and there was no way he was going to let him go.

Eventually, prompted by a sense of threat and a message from the Lord (Genesis 31:1-3), Jacob and his household made a run for it, only to be caught eventually by Laban at the hill country of Gilead. It was here that a fascinating confrontation took place. Laban wanted Jacob and all he owned back where he believed they belonged, and his language reflected his sense of ownership:

"The women are my daughters, the children are my children, and the flocks are my flocks. All you see is mine. Yet what can I do today about these daughters of mine, or about the children they have borne?" (Genesis 31:43)

Laban pushed for control and played one last desperate card in the hope that Jacob would crack under pressure and return back home. But Jacob did not budge nor bend. So strong was his resolve and response, that Laban was forced to make a face-saving agreement that allowed both men to go where they needed to go. Note Laban's final language to Jacob:

"Here is this heap, and here is this pillar I have set up between you and me. This heap is a witness, and this pillar is a witness, that I will not go past this heap to your side to harm you and that you will not go past this heap and pillar to my side to harm me…" (Genesis 31:51-53)

With the use of 'ābar, translated here as "go past", the two men were not simply making an agreement, but creating a border – one that neither would pass over. Laban would never again encroach into Jacob's world and Jacob would never again return to Paddan Aram and Laban's domain. The text shows the two men never met again. This was an agreement of closure and by making it, Jacob declared that he would no longer be driven by the agenda of another.

Interestingly, when the men departed from each other the next day, the Torah notes that Laban kissed his two daughters and his grandchildren and blessed them. But it seems he did not bless Jacob!

Did Laban withhold his blessing because he could no longer control his nephew?

Torah's echo here may be a little harder to hear, but nonetheless it speaks. Just like her brother, Rebekah had in effect taken control of Jacob's destiny by making key decisions on his behalf and by getting him to do what she wanted.

"Now, my son, listen carefully and do what I tell you." (Genesis 27:8)

"My son, let the curse fall on me. Just do what I say…" (Genesis 27:13)

"Then Rebekah… put them (Esau's clothes) on her younger son… she also covered his hands…" (Genesis 27:15-16)

"Now then, my son, do what I say: Flee at once…" (Genesis 27:43)

"I'll send word for you to come back from there…" (Genesis 27:45)

Though Rebekah's motivation toward Jacob, and that of her brother Laban's, were poles apart, the end result looked and sounded almost the same. In both cases, two strong people had very clear ideas on what Jacob's life should look like, and both sought to control who he was, what he did and where he went. Jacob had failed to resist the relentless force of his mother, but eventually he stood up to her brother by refusing to wear the clothes Laban chose for him and by escaping over the boundary Laban had created for him. In surrendering to Rebekah, Jacob was forced into exile, but because he stood up to Laban, Jacob was able to return home.

Rebekah *dominated* her son Jacob, but Jacob refused to be dominated by his Uncle Laban.

What do we learn from Jacob's exilic experience?

Running never brings resolution
When we run, the only thing that changes is our address. For a while, everything will feel good, with new surroundings and a fresh start,

but eventually the unresolved issues that caused us to run in the first place will re-emerge, and we'll find ourselves back in the same room, even if the furniture has changed.

Remember, the Lord can run faster than we can and He's already where we are going before we get there. Running will satisfy short-term fear, but it is not the answer to the issues that drove us to start running. When we run it gives us the impression we are in control, captains of our own destiny... but we're not, or we wouldn't be running.

It's time to stop running from your God-shaped identity and from your God-designed purpose, and it's time to surrender to Him, liberating the person He made you to be, even in the *space in-between*.

We are where we need to be not where we want to be
Sometimes we find ourselves in places we didn't plan to be and certainly don't want to stay, yet no matter how hard we try, we can't seem to escape. Having run once, we try it again, only to find that the exits are barred and the roads out are blocked. Frustration rises and we come to hate where we are and everything associated with it. Yet, maybe, just maybe, the "Paddan Aram" we find ourselves in can become the place where reality is confronted; where instead of trying to escape the landscape, we embrace the lessons.

Remember, the Lord is not hindered by borders, boundaries or walls; He can work as effectively in Paddan Aram as He can in heaven. Human postcodes don't intimidate Him and checkpoints can't stop Him, for He is able to work in the most unlikely of places to produce the most unexpected results.

It's time to stop cursing and criticising the *space in-between* and start inviting the Lord of heaven into it. He's there already... but your invite for Him to come in will open your eyes to the reality He has been in all along.

How you see where you are will determine how you live there!

Laban might be the Lord in disguise

Over the years there have been people in my world who I never wanted to leave and others (only a few in comparison), that I didn't want to stay. You know the type I mean, the people who provoke, agitate, argue and generally make life more unpleasant than it needs to be. Most times I've been able to control their influence in my life by simply shutting them out, but there have been seasons when pulling down the shutters on them was impossible and, for one reason or another, they weren't going away. I am not saying these people were from the Lord, although some of them claimed to be, but I found that at the very least, the Lord used them in specific ways to expose, challenge, provoke and produce things in me and through me. At times I wanted to tell those "Labans" where to go and if I could have replaced them, I would gladly have done so. Yet now I look back and see the hand of the Lord in their agency and the purpose of the Lord being perfected through their provocation.

Remember, even *Laban* can be a vehicle for the Lord! The boss you hate, the neighbour you struggle with, the relative who without fail, empties your tank, can all be *Labans*, forcing us to confront who we are (and who we're not) and pushing us towards our purpose. Your *Laban* may never become a friend, but they might be a tool in the hand of heaven.

It's time to stop fighting *Laban* and start embracing what he's potentially teaching you. One day you will leave him behind, but today, in the *space in-between,* he forms part of the fabric of your world and should not be ignored.

The *space in-between* was both prosperous and painful for Jacob. His family enlarged, but with it so did the seeds of fracture, nurtured in the soil of favouritism. His wealth increased, but not without the lurking presence of agendas and a strain on relationships. He grew as a man, coming to terms with his own God-shaped identity and perhaps the realisation, crystalized through his own disappointments, that just as the actions of others had bestowed pain and sorrow on him in the *space in-between*, so his own actions towards Esau, Isaac and Rebekah had left a legacy of brokenness that, in the liminal place, he had come to regret. Paddan Aram was never meant to be Jacob's final destination, but the Lord used the years he spent living there to work on his wayward son, for the Lord didn't just want Jacob to *return*, but wanted *Jacob* to return! If the real, authentic, true Jacob returned, then a moment could be created where His Maker could meet him face to face, and call out of the grasper the prince who lived within. As he crossed the border back into the Land of Promise, Jacob did so without disguise or pretence. Laban disappeared from his rear-view mirror and Esau now loomed just over the horizon. As Jacob prepared himself for an encounter with his brother he could not avoid, the Lord was preparing an encounter with Jacob that he could not imagine.

Take a moment to reflect on the following questions:

Are there experiences in your life which are an echo of what has been before? Is the echo a call to resolve something within rather than run from it?

Are there coincidences in your life that may well be God-incidences? Maybe the presence of those God-incidences is an indication that He has not given up on you.

Part 2 – The Face of Authenticity

Chapter 8 – What is Your Name?

Genesis 32:22-32

The Lord loves asking questions. In fact, the first recorded conversation the Lord had with humans started with a question,[1] and that pattern continued throughout the whole of the Tanakh. Next time you read any passages containing dialogue between the Lord and people in the Old Testament, check out how many questions He asked – it will amaze you. As we move into the New Testament, Jesus, the Son of God in human form, followed the exact same pattern. Throughout the record of the four Gospels it is estimated that Jesus asked 307 questions, while answering only three.[2] Again, the next time you're in the Gospels, just highlight in your Bible every time Jesus asked a question. Here are some examples:

"Can any one of you by worrying add a single hour to your life?" (Matthew 6:27)

"To what can I compare this generation?" (Matthew 11:16)

"Who is my mother, and who are my brothers?" (Matthew 12:48)

"'You of little faith,' he said, 'why did you doubt?'" (Matthew 14:31)

"And why do you break the command of God for the sake of your tradition?" (Matthew 15:3)

"How many loaves do you have?" (Matthew 15:34)

"Who do you say I am?" (Matthew 16:15)

---

1. Genesis 3:9
2. Martin, B. Copenhaver, *Jesus is the Question*, Abingdon Press, 2014

It seems the Lord is very inquisitive, and these are just some of the questions He asked in Matthew.

Genesis 32 describes the encounter between Jacob and a mysterious "man". When the man[3] wrestled with Jacob in the garden that night, He asked him an innocuous question:

"What is your name?" (Genesis 32:27)[4]

If this was the Lord, or even a representative of the Lord, He knew the name of the man He wrestled with. The question didn't reveal anything lacking in the Lord's omniscience, rather it was intended to throw a spotlight on the veracity of Jacob's answer. The symmetry between this event in Genesis 32 and the one we've spent considerable time reflecting on in Genesis 27 is unmissable.

Just as Jacob was alone before his father, Isaac, so he is now alone before the Lord. Just as he wanted something from his father, he wanted, even needed something from the Lord. Just as Isaac, through the fog of his dim eyes, probed his son with three questions in search of truth and trust, so the Lord, though all-seeing and all-knowing, jabbed His finger into the depths of Jacob's soul with only one question. As we discovered back in chapter 5, because Isaac could not see, he relied on the truth of what he was told, and because he did not know who was before him, he relied on the trustworthiness of that individual. In the distant past, Jacob had taken advantage of the vulnerability of his father, but now before the Lord who knows and sees, Jacob faced another question!

Why did the Lord ask the question?

The clear and obvious answer will be the focus of this and subsequent chapters as we consider the *face of truth*.

---

3. The Hebrew text describes the person as "a man", but later Jacob, when trying to understand what happened, clearly believed he had encountered the Lord. So, from this moment on, I will take Jacob's lead and assume the man was the Lord.
4. It is striking that in the whole of the discourse between Himself and Jacob, the Lord asked two questions and both related to identity (see verse 29).

But before we jump into this, may I suggest, that part of the reason for asking this question was as much about Jacob's past, as it was about his future.

The Question was a Reminder

I don't think Jacob needed reminding of the day that he betrayed his father and cheated his brother. Even his behaviour recorded in the earlier part of chapter 32 shows that Jacob was still living with, and very aware of, what he had done to Esau. When he eventually met his brother, his language and behaviour was humility personified.[5]

Could it be that when the Lord asked Jacob his name, he heard the voice of his father ask,

"Who is it?" (Genesis 27:18)

The answer to that question had set in motion a chain of events that took Jacob far from home and the Land of Promise. Of all the questions the Lord could have asked Jacob that night, He asked this one because He was reminding Jacob of the power of a lie and the tyranny of pretence. In the echo of Isaac's question, the Lord issued him a warning: answer carefully… answer truthfully!

The Question demanded a Return

On the surface, this was the easiest of questions for Jacob to answer, but we must remember that names, especially in a biblical cultural context, are rarely just about labels. They are often linked to identity and purpose, saturated with meaning and intent. We know that Jacob was given the name "one who grasps", because he was born grasping his brother's heel. Even Esau acknowledged that he was well named.

In front of his father, Jacob had taken the name of his brother:

"I am Esau your first born." (Genesis 27:19)

---

5. Genesis 33:1-15

To attain what he wanted, he believed he had to become someone else to get it, so he covered himself, hid the truth of who he was, and in a moment of pressure and scrutiny, became another. As the Lord's question rang out that night, a deeper question resounded within his heart: *who would Jacob be before the face of heaven?* Would he return to type, reach for a disguise, come up with a plan and try to pull the wool over the Shepherd's eyes? The question forced Jacob to return to a day when he became someone else, but now he was challenged by the Lord to be himself and take his chances with the truth.

The Question offered a Release

The next words out of Jacob's mouth would determine his future and influence the destiny of millions who would follow. He, of course, did not know what that would be, but I suspect he understood this question was neither random nor coincidental. This was not a trick from the Lord or a cruel trap to ensnare the grasper. Rather, this was a question that offered redemption from the past and release into a future beyond his dreams. The Lord did not ask the question to punish his wandering son, but to get him back on track, and call out of him the God-shaped identity that had always been within.

When Jacob answered "I am," to his father's final question many years before, he had believed the *blessing* would open up a door of opportunity and success, but instead it became a burden he was not designed to carry and one he was quick to return when reunited with his brother Esau:

"'Please accept *the present* that was brought to you, for God has been gracious to me and I have all I need.' And because Jacob insisted, Esau accepted it." (Genesis 33:11)

The word translated "present" in the NIV is actually *berākāh*, better translated *blessing* – the same word used of Isaac when he exclaimed to Esau:

"Your brother came deceitfully and took your *blessing*." (Genesis 27:35)

Is this a coincidence? Could it be that when Jacob offered his blessing to Esau he was returning what he had stolen from him? Having lived with it for many years, had he realised that what he had achieved and received through disguise and deceit he was never supposed to have?

Two things may support this idea. Firstly, the contrast between the language of chapter 33, verses 10 and 11:

"'No, please!' said Jacob. 'If I have found favour in your eyes, accept this *gift* from me. For to see your face is like seeing the face of God, now that you have received me favourably.'"

In verse 10 he says "accept this gift" and the word he used here was *minḥāh*, pointing to the idea of a gift, a tribute or an offering. Yet, in the very next verse, although it sounds to us as though he is talking about the same thing, he changes the word. Was his shift from *gift* to *blessing* deliberate?

Secondly, consider his words to Esau as he concludes,

"...for God has been gracious to me and I have all I need."

Is this an echo back to Isaac's *second blessing* to Jacob (or the first, when he knew it was actually Jacob)?

"May God Almighty bless you and make you fruitful and increase your numbers until you become a community of peoples. May he give you and your descendants the blessing given to Abraham, so that you may take possession of the land where you now reside as a foreigner, the land God gave to Abraham." (Genesis 28:3-4)

Isaac's blessing is an accurate description of how Jacob returned and what he was about to do in purchasing some of the Land of Promise. Perhaps Jacob understood *which blessing* he was meant to carry and why. Maybe his wrestling bout with God the night before meeting Esau was simply a confirmation of this truth. The Lord asked the question not to trap Jacob in the past, but to lead him into a glorious and world-changing future. But no matter how magnificent the intention behind the question, everything hinged on the answer.

So how did he answer?

Jacob's posture that night was as important as his proclamation, and we cannot consider what he said without framing his answer in the context of his attitudes. That night, three dynamic attributes combined in Jacob to create an irresistible fragrance for the Lord; attributes which Scripture shows us, the Lord both loves and responds to.

Humility

The Torah highlights this with a simple description of the moment:

"So Jacob was left alone…" (Genesis 32:24)

When he stood before his father Isaac, Jacob went in alone, sent by his mother. Now he was alone by choice, having sent his family across the stream. Jacob made the choice to be alone because he understood that something needed to happen for which he could not rely on another, nor be tempted to reach for the many tools within his innovative box. He was now alone without family, without friends, without wealth and without a clever exit plan.

His humility was expressed earlier when, on hearing of Esau's approach, he prayed:

"I am unworthy of all the kindness and faithfulness You have shown Your servant. I had only a staff when I crossed this Jordan, but now I have become two groups." (Genesis 32:10)

The humility with which he returned to the land is in stark contrast to the attitude with which he exited, even after an encounter with God in Luz, a place he renamed *Bet'El*, house of God.[6] But we will return to the significance of that event in a later chapter. Conscious

---

6. Genesis 28:10-22

of the Lord's goodness to him and his own vulnerability and sense of weakness, Jacob now waits for God... *alone*!

The Lord loves humility

The New Testament tell us:

"All of you, clothe yourselves with humility toward one another, because, 'God opposes the proud but shows favour to the humble.' Humble yourselves, therefore, under God's mighty hand, that He may lift you up in due time." (1 Peter 5:5-6)

The word for humility used repeatedly through this passage is *tapeinóo* and carries with it the idea of making oneself low. Peter urges the called-out followers of Jesus to make themselves low towards each other, but more importantly before the Lord. He argues that when the Lord sees humility, and when we voluntarily and willingly make ourselves low before Him, He responds by lifting that person up to a place they could not have attained alone. By contrast the Lord *arranges Himself against*[7] those who *raise or inflate themselves* above their station.[8]

As we contrast Jacob before Isaac and his posture before the Lord, we observe an *arrogant alone* in Genesis 27 – a young man who audaciously entered the presence of his father and three times "inflated himself" above his brother, his God and his father. As Jacob lifted himself up, he manifested an attitude that God resisted and even hated:

"There are six things the Lord hates,
seven that are detestable to him:
haughty eyes, a lying tongue,
hands that shed innocent blood,

---

7. antitásso -*anti*, against, and *tásso*, to arrange.
8. huperéphanos, from *hupér*, over, above, and *phaino*, to shine, show.

a heart that devises wicked schemes,
feet that are quick to rush into evil,
a false witness who pours out lies
and a person who stirs up conflict in the community."
(Proverbs 6:16-19)

Before Isaac, we might conclude that Jacob ticked a lot, if not everything, on this list! But notice specifically "haughty eyes", the first of the seven – maybe because it is a gateway to the others. The word used here is *rûm*, a verb which means "to raise, lift up and be exalted", a perfect description of the grasper before his father.

But look now at Jacob as he sits alone waiting for God. This is not a man exalting himself, but one who has bowed himself low and who is now exactly where the Lord wants him. Humbled and bowed low, Jacob's attitude issued an invitation to the Almighty to come and lift the grasper up!

Humility is the gateway to freedom, not only before the Lord, but within ourselves. "Haughty eyes" will always take us further than we should go and tempt us to become what we are not. When we inflate ourselves we become, at best, a distorted reflection of our true self and, at worst, an impoverished version of someone else. Haughty eyes will always take us away from the Lord and convince us that we know best, while the arrogance that pride breeds will set us up in opposition to the One who has a better plan for us in His hands.

If we bow low before Him, He will lift us up!

Hunger

Jacob's hunger and desperation for an answer and a breakthrough are seen in three things.

Firstly, in his wrestling.

Not only is this the first reference to wrestling in the Torah, it's the only one. So great was Jacob's hunger for the Lord that he entered into a whole new experience and engaged with the Lord in a way that no one had ever done before. What makes it even more remarkable is that we are told,

"…a man wrestled with him till daybreak." (v24)

It's not clear from the text when the wrestling bout started, but one thing is sure, it lasted a significant time. This was not a fleeting moment of encounter, but a relentless, painful, exhausting and all-encompassing engagement.

Secondly, in his response

Jacob wrestled so tenaciously with the Lord, that in an attempt to break free of his grasp, the Lord dislocated Jacob's hip. Crippling pain would have exploded into Jacob's body as bone that normally nestled in the socket it was designed for, now grated against another bone. Yet incredibly, with one leg out of action and experiencing unimaginable discomfort, as the text tells us…

"…his hip was wrenched as he wrestled with the man." (v25)

…Jacob kept wrestling! His hunger was such that even the pain barrier did not stop him.

Thirdly, in his request

"I will not let You go unless You bless me." (v26)

There is possibly a beautiful play on the Hebrew word used by Jacob. When he asks the Lord to bless him, the word is *bārak,* and its meaning contains not only the idea of blessing and greeting, but of saluting and even kneeling. With his hip dislocated, Jacob must have fallen, held up only by the strength of his arms and his ability to hop on one leg. But as he fell, could it be that he *knelt* and leaned into the

Lord, sweat pouring from a brow buried into the Lord's chest, his legs shaking and wobbling from adrenalin and pain. As his good knee bent, he cried out for blessing!

The Lord loves hunger

In proclaiming what the Kingdom of God looked like, Jesus declared,

"Blessed are those who hunger and thirst for righteousness, for they will be filled." (Matthew 5:6)

In the Kingdom, it is not the strongest, the best, the brightest and the most gifted who get filled, rather, it is the hungry, whoever they may be. So many times, as my children were growing up, I saw them pick at wonderful home-cooked food and leave plates half finished. When asked if there was a problem, the reply was usually, "I've already eaten." There was nothing wrong with the food, how it was prepared or arranged – the issue was the appetite of my children. Food always tastes better when we're hungry and even great food isn't that attractive when we've nibbled on other things!

The hunger of Jacob before his father Isaac was fuelled by selfish ambition. He wanted to be his brother, he wanted to have the blessing and he wanted to be better than he was. Jacob's desperation to be more, placed *self* at the centre and hurt everyone it touched. His hunger was all about satisfying self. But now, look at the man clinging onto the Lord, dripping with sweat, every joint and muscle aching with pain. Yet, he held on, not just for himself but because he understood something greater was at stake. The outcome of this night would impact his wives, his children and the community of people that lay within them. Jacob was not simply grasping for self, but for them.

Hunger for the Lord is the pathway to greatness, as we let go of what we want and lay hold of Him. We realise that without Him, who we are will not be enough. But with Him, who we are will be enough and more. Don't let a world that offers much but delivers little of true value ruin your appetite for Him. Stay hungry and thirsty for Him, for only then can we be filled supernaturally and truly satisfied.

Honesty

When the Lord asked Jacob his name, his response was emphatic and uncompromising. In one breath, one word and one moment of naked truth, decades of guilt vanished, as the grasper shouted,

"Jacob." (v27)

There's no exclamation mark but if feels to me like there should be. He doesn't say "I am Jacob," just "Jacob"! Note the contrast to his responses to Isaac:

"I am Esau your firstborn." (Genesis 27:19)

When asked if he was really Isaac's son he replied:

"I am." (Genesis 27:24)

These responses are measured, crafted and carefully executed. But when the Lord asked his name, years of frustration exploded in raw and honest passion: "Jacob"! Was the pain of his dislocated hip speaking or maybe the exhaustion of a long night of wrestling? These may indeed have factored, but I suspect that this question, a reminder of another question, a return to a place of deceit and duplicity, offered Jacob a moment of truth and release that he took without hesitation as he told the Lord something He already knew! The Lord knew Jacob was Jacob, but now, with such an emphatic answer, the Lord knew that *Jacob knew* he was Jacob.

The Lord loves honesty

That's why His first words to Adam after the fall were in the form of a question.

That's why He asked Cain why he was so angry and later where his brother Abel was.

That's why He asked Abraham why Sarah laughed.

That's why He asked Israel why they thought their way was hidden from Him.

That's why Jesus asked people if they wanted to get well.

That's why Jesus asked Peter if he loved Him.

The Lord already knows the answer, but He wants to know if we know and if we will have the courage to let Him into our lives, through moments of naked and transformational honesty. The Lord doesn't ask the question for His sake, but for ours, for it is not the question He is interested in. Rather, He longs for an answer of truth that gives Him permission to fill us, bless us and call something more out of us that can only emerge when we stop pretending and embrace the God-shaped *Jacob* we are.

Just as Jacob's disguise and deceit before his father set off a chain reaction decades before, so this one truthful answer before the Lord enabled Him to do something in and through Jacob that has impacted and enriched billions of people across the earth. Having experienced through Jesus the fruit of the blessing given to Jacob, I for one am glad he was honest that night – and that when the Lord asked him the simplest of questions he gave the right answer. From that moment, everything changed for him… and for us!

The Lord loves humility, for when we bow low before Him, He can lift us up higher than we could have imagined possible.

The Lord loves hunger, for when we feast on Him, He can satisfy us as only a supernatural God can.

The Lord loves honesty, for when we have the courage to be truthful with Him, He has the power to transform us and call from us everything planted in our God-shaped original design.

When He asks your name, tell Him the truth!

Take a moment to reflect on the following questions:

How can humility help us when it comes to an understanding of who we are and the purpose of our lives?

What factors impact your hunger for the Lord?

Honesty before the Lord is the most liberating experience a human can have. Take the time to sit in His presence and tell Him your name. He already knows, but He wants to know if you know!

Chapter 9 – From Jacob to Israel

Genesis 32:22-32

As the sun rose over Penuel that morning, it was the signal of a new day, in more ways than one. Jacob emerged from a night of *combat* with both bruises and a blessing, limping toward his destiny with a brand-new name. But it would be a mistake to believe that these *gifts* bestowed on Jacob were the product of only one moment of encounter. Too often this night has been seen as a stand-alone event, when it must be understood not only in the context of his entire journey thus far, but with specific reference to the day he stood before his father Isaac and audaciously declared himself to be someone else.

Deceit had launched Jacob to a land not his own, but now, his raw, naked, passionate honesty, gave the Lord permission not only to establish him in the land promised to his grandfather and father, but to commission him and the people within him to the purpose for which the Lord had called them. Jacob's humility, hunger and honesty, forged over years of struggle and frustration, formed the fertile soil in which the seeds of transformation were planted and from which salvation to the nations would grow. Jacob learnt that night, and teaches us today, that *the Lord will not transform the person we're pretending to be, only the person we are!*

Of all the name changes in the Bible, Jacob's stands out as possibly the most dramatic. We have in the Scriptures some beautiful examples of a person's name being changed. Abram (exalted father) became Abraham (father of many).[1] Jonathan (the Lord has given) became Shuvael (the returned of God).[2] Simon (God hears) became Peter (rock)[3] and Joseph (the Lord adds) became Barnabas (son of consolation or encouragement).[4] Although all of these changes are significant in their own right, the nature of their changes are pedestrian in comparison to the dynamic context of Jacob's. Two names changed as a result of that night – the name of the man struggling with the God and the place in which they struggled. We'll return to the significance of the place name in the next chapter, but for now, let us consider the significance of the change in Jacob.

His new name was about something *within* him

Jacob was given a brand new name and its mention in Genesis 32:28 is the first time in the Torah that this name was spoken by God and heard by a human.[5] His new name was Israel, (*yiśrā'ēl*), and although in English we understand it as one word, it has three components, two of which we'll look at now. The first part of the word to consider is *yiśrā'ēl*, a verb that has at its heart the meaning of struggle – an idea emphasised cleverly later in the verse when it says, "because you have *struggled*" (*śārāh*). The second part is *yiśrā'ēl*, meaning "he", and points to the subject of the verb, namely "he struggles". From the construction and the context, it is generally accepted that the "he" here is Jacob, therefore he is the one doing the struggling.

If we accept that Jacob is the *he* doing the struggling, then we are drawn again into a remarkable echo and sense of providential symmetry. The name Jacob, "grasper", is changed to a name that has

1. Genesis 17:5
2. 1 Chronicles 23:16 and Judges 18:30-31
3. John 1:42 - renamed by Jesus
4. Acts 4:36 - renamed by the apostles
5. It's Genesis 32:29 in the Hebrew Bible

the idea of struggle at its heart. Could it be that though new, this name was not something randomly plucked out of the air, nor simply a description of the experience of its recipient that night? Could it be that what the Lord named that night was a grown-up version of the baby jostling in his mother's womb,[6] grasping his brother's heel? If that is the case, then the Lord was giving a new name to describe someone who was already there. He was not imposing a new identity on Jacob, but redeeming a lost one. From the moment he was conceived, Jacob was Israel, he just never knew it until now!

Just as the Lord called Abraham out of Abram and Jesus called Peter out of Simon, so God called Israel out of Jacob! The Lord called these names out, and by doing so, the original person He shaped and the destiny He designed. They were humans named Abram, Simon and Jacob, but it was the Lord who called Abraham, Peter and Israel out of them.

In describing the Servant of the Lord Isaiah writes,

"Before I was born the Lord called me; from my mother's womb He has spoken my name." (Isaiah 49:1)

Look closely at the detail, for we have someone *called* before they were born and *named* while still in the womb. Jacob was called and named long before he understood what any of that meant, but that night in the garden, the God who called and named him eventually caught up with him.

There is a call upon us and a name within us that has nothing to do with our parents, heritage, culture, colour or background. What our circumstances, context or community has conferred upon us or named us, is not necessarily *who we are* or *why we are here*. Whatever our beginnings, whether they be good, bad or ugly; whatever our journey, whether it is something we're proud of or ashamed of, the Lord wants to redeem our God-designed call and our God-given

---

6. rāṣaṣ – to crush or oppress

name. The adversary of our souls and the stuff of life will attempt to define us by distorting our name and destroying our destiny, but the God who called Israel out of Jacob that night, longs to call a new name out of us.

"Therefore, if anyone is in Christ, he is a new creation. The old has passed away; behold, the new has come." (2 Corinthians 5:17)[7]

His new name was about something *above him*

Let's return to the name Israel and consider the third and most important part, namely, *yisra͗ʾel,* which means God. The outstanding difference between Jacob's given name and that gifted by God is the presence of God within the name. His new name could therefore be understood as "he struggles *with* God". However, there is debate around how this is to be interpreted. Is Jacob struggling with God or is God struggling with Jacob? Is it pointing towards human struggle or divine struggle? As suggested earlier in this chapter, the weight of opinion leans to the former idea, namely, that he (Jacob) struggled with God. But we should not forget that Jacob only got to struggle with God, because the Lord *wrestled* with him!

"So Jacob was left alone, and a man wrestled with him till daybreak." (Genesis 32:24)

Here clearly, it is *the man* wrestling with Jacob, and though Jacob struggled back and prevailed, he only got to do so because *the man* took the initiative and took hold of him.[8]

I love this idea, for without the insertion of verse 24, we might conclude that it was Jacob's wrestling on its own that achieved the result. Therefore, we might be tempted to conclude that the name Israel was a reward for human endeavour and achievement.

---

7. ESV
8. 'abaq – as referenced previously, this is the only time this verb is used in the Scriptures to describe the actions of *the man.*

However, the truth remains that although Jacob struggled, he got to do so because the Lord wrestled. Without the Lord's grace in coming to him, no amount of graft and grit on Jacob's part could have achieved such an amazing outcome. Jacob got to be Israel because the Lord desperately wanted his wayward grasper to become His prince among the nations. His grace made glory possible!

"But now, this is what the Lord says – He who created you, Jacob, He who formed you, Israel: 'Do not fear, for I have redeemed you; I have summoned you by name; you are Mine.'" (Isaiah 43:1)

Look at the grace details within this wonderful text:

"who created you"

"who formed you"

"I have redeemed you"

"I have summoned you"

Whoever we are to become and whatever we may get to do, we must never forget that it is only possible because the Lord, in grace, initiated the process and reached out to us. We get to struggle with Him because He first wrestled for us, and we get to prevail because He is determined never to let us go. We serve a God who is both overflowing in grace and relentless in faithfulness. When we did not deserve it or even ask for it, He came to us in our aloneness and brokenness and took hold of us, in order to call out of us His name and empower us to carry His purpose across the earth.

It is easy to forget that He did it first, especially when we prosper and life is good, but we must never forget that Israel only emerged out of Jacob because God made it so. In grace He comes to us to wrestle for our souls, and in faithfulness He remains with us as He struggles for our surrender. Perhaps when we understand that He was looking for us long before we were looking for Him, so that He might liberate us into the fullness of our identity and destiny, we might be more willing to surrender, not just to struggle!

"For it is by grace you have been saved, through faith – and this is not from yourselves, it is the gift of God – not by works, so that no one can boast. For we are God's workmanship, created in Christ Jesus to do good works, which God prepared in advance for us to do." (Ephesians 2:8-10)

His new name was about something *beyond him*

Jacob's name change was never only about him, but about a plan in the heart of God that lay beyond the boundary of one individual. God's dream was spoken to his grandfather:

"...and all peoples on earth will be blessed through you." (Genesis 12:2-3)

It was repeated to his father:

"...and through your offspring all nations on earth will be blessed..." (Genesis 26:2-5)

Now, in this new name, the Divine dream would begin to become a reality, as out of Israel a community would arise through which the nations would be blessed and enriched. Jacob's name change was not just about who he was, but about the purpose connected to that identity – an identity called out, enhanced and liberated in the name Israel! I'm not sure Jacob fully understood all of this as he limped from his encounter with the Lord, but later on, when the Lord brought him back to Bethel (an episode we'll consider in the next chapter), He not only confirmed Jacob's change of name, but the ideas at the heart of that change.

Genesis 35:9-12 summaries all three ideas brilliantly:

"After Jacob returned from Paddan Aram, God appeared to him again and blessed him. God said to him, 'Your name is Jacob, but you will no longer be called Jacob; your name will be Israel.' So He named him Israel. And God said to him, 'I am God Almighty; be fruitful and increase in number. A nation and a community of nations will come from you, and kings will be among your descendants. The land I gave to Abraham and Isaac I also give to you, and I will give this land to your descendants after you.'"

Note that the Lord reminded him of his new name, and it is interesting that Jacob is referenced twice as is Israel, as if to make sure he's got the point. Jacob is being urged by the Lord to own his new name, because by embracing it he will embrace much more than a name. Look at the detail of verses 10-12:

"…you will no longer be called Jacob; your name will be Israel…" (v10)

His new name was about something *within him.*

"I am God Almighty…" (v11)

His new name was about something *above him.*

"A nation and a community of nations will come from you, and kings will come from your body." (v11)

"…and I will give this land to your descendants after you." (v12)

His new name was about something *beyond him.*

The heart of the Lord resounded through the words of the prophet Isaiah, when in seeking to restore Israel He declared,

"…I will also make you a light for the Gentiles, that you may bring My salvation to the ends of the earth." (Isaiah 49:6)

Jacob's new name contained within it the name of God, so the mandate inherent within the name was to carry God and His salvation to the nations of the world. The Lord didn't simply want to save Jacob that night, He wanted to save the world through Jacob! If Jacob owned his new name, then the Lord would realise His dream.

The name given to us in Christ Jesus, the Seed of Abraham, and the embodiment of God's heart for the world in human flesh, carries not only Divine meaning but Divine purpose. He has not redeemed us and given us a new name so that we can simply and selfishly enjoy the benefits of our position, but so that we can be a blessing to the world by embracing our purpose… *His dream!*

Having been made new we therefore understand and embrace the fact that,

"We are therefore Christ's ambassadors, as though God were making His appeal through us." (2 Corinthians 5:20)

Having been lavished with grace when the Lord came to us, we therefore understand and embrace fact that,

"His intent was that now, through the Church [His called out community], the manifold wisdom of God should be made known…" (Ephesians 3:10)

The pursuit of God-shaped identity and with it an understanding of God-designed destiny will never simply be about an individual. Rather it will always be about the facilitation of His dream to touch the world through those who have been transformed by Him. If we will have the courage to move the narrative away from "who I am" and "what I want", and centre it on the truth of "who God is" and "what He wants", then His wrestling for us and our struggle with Him will not be in vain. Let us not allow encounter with Him to be reduced to our experience of Him, but may our struggle with Him bring us so close to Him, so that we experience the grip of His grace, feel His breath on our face, and know the beat of His heart, so that we leave changed and determined to carry Him to our world.

Jacob's story is our story! Born into a world where to grasp is both encouraged and expected, humans find themselves surrounded by and saturated with the mantra that *self is god*. We are inextricably driven by the need to defend, enhance and advance self, regardless of the cost to us or those around us. But as we grasp for self, there is a Lord in heaven who struggles with us and for us. His desire is to call us back from the futility and emptiness of self-advancement, to a place of willing submission to His reign and plan; to a heart that is prepared to surrender the god of self to the Lord of heaven! This rarely happens without struggle as our will comes into conflict with His will, and although He will never violate our freedom to choose, He will contend, struggle and fight for us and with us. He fights because He knows there is a greater name within us and a bigger call upon us, having formed them both in us before we left our mother's womb.

Take a moment to reflect on the following questions:

What name have people and/or circumstances attributed to us that works against what the Lord calls us? Are there any names that you have received that you should not own?

Perhaps you've been told, "your success is determined by your struggle", and this has placed pressure on you in your walk with God. Is it time to reflect on His grace – that we only get to struggle with Him because He came to wrestle with us?

Have you reduced your walk with God and your understanding of your purpose down to being something that is only about you? Surrender to the truth that who you are and what you are called to do will always be about something much bigger than you.

Chapter 10 - From House to Face

Genesis 28:10-22
Genesis 32:22-32
Genesis 35:1-15

Jacob's name was not the only name to change as a result of his encounter with God. Just as the Lord named him, he in turn gave a new name to the place. He called it *peniyʻel*, meaning "face of God", as he concluded so beautifully:

"It is because I saw God *face to face*, and yet my life was spared." (32:30)

Though this is the first time the phrase "face to face" (*pāniym ʻel pāniym*) appears in the Torah, the idea at the heart of this magnificent and glorious statement runs like a golden thread throughout the Scriptures. We see the nuance of this idea in the creation of the first human:

"Then the Lord God formed a man from the dust of the ground and breathed into his nostrils the breath of life, and the man became a living being." (Genesis 2:7)

The image here is remarkable: as a fully formed man lies on the ground, made out of the dust that forms his bed, and though visibly human, he lacks one thing: namely *life* itself. So, the Lord "…breathed into his nostrils…" and the man became a living being. But before we rush off, let's pause to embrace the image before us. For in order for God to breathe into the man, He had to come down to where the man was and get close enough to allow His breath to enter the man's nose. The first human came to life because of a *face to face* encounter with God!

A few years ago, my wife and I went to Rome for our wedding anniversary and, like many others, we signed up for a tour around the Vatican – an experience I found both inspiring and disturbing. Our lovely Italian guide (who loved addressing us as "my darlings"), became very excited as we were about to enter the Sistine Chapel. Before we went in, he gathered us into a huddle and in hushed tones spoke to us about Michelangelo's amazing work, and in particular his own favourite piece, The Creation of Adam. If you're not familiar with the painting, Google it, and you'll see how Michelangelo envisaged this creation moment. In it, God (complete with flowing grey hair and long grey beard), is reaching out His hand towards Adam (who is very naked) and in turn is reaching out to God. One of God's fingers is stretching to a finger that Adam has extended, and the implication is that Divine life passed to the man from God, from finger to finger! I discovered that day that Michelangelo was an amazing artist, but a rubbish theologian! Nothing could be further from the truth and what a tragic depiction of such a world-shaping moment. The first human was not created by a force emitted from a finger, but by breath from *The Face*. This was not an impersonal power transaction, but something that was intended to be understood as personal, tender and intimate. As the man opened his eyes for the first time, the first thing he saw was the face of God! This was how the Lord made us, because this is how the Lord wants us: *face to face*.

Long after Jacob was gathered to his fathers, the Lord redeemed His people out of slavery, led by Moses. As they began their journey through the wilderness, the Torah tell us that Moses built a "tent of meeting" – a place where the people could go and inquire of God, and there something remarkable happened:

"The Lord would speak to Moses *face to face*, as one speaks to a friend." (Exodus 33:11)

The phrase here is identical to that spoken by Jacob at Peniel.

But the Lord didn't just want Moses to have this experience, His heart was to speak *face to face* with His people:

"The Lord spoke to you (plural) *face to face* out of the fire on the mountain." (Deuteronomy 5:4)

The Lord didn't remain on the mountain, but came down to dwell with the people in a Tabernacle (*miškān* – dwelling place), made especially for Him, placed at the centre of the camp, symbolically depicting a *face to face* relationship with His people.

Hundreds of years later, the Lord who lived in the *miškān* tented Himself among humans in a completely unique and radical way:

"The Word became flesh and made His *dwelling among us*. We have *seen* His glory, the glory of the One and only Son, who came from the Father, full of grace and truth." (John 1:14)

The phrase translated "dwelling among us" comes from the word *skēnóō*, pointing to the idea of God "pitching a tent" and "encamping" among us through the incarnation of Jesus. John added "...we have seen His glory...", for just as Moses saw God *face to face* in *his* tent, John declared we have seen and beheld Him *face to face* because of *His Tent*. As if to reinforce this idea, John expounds on this imagery in his first letter when he writes:

"That which was from the beginning, which we have *heard*,[1] which we have *seen*[2] with our eyes, which we have *looked at*[3] and our hands

---

1. *akoúō* – to hear someone or something. It is used twice in this passage.
2. *horáō* – to see in a way as to perceive; to understand through the eyes. It is used three times in the passage.
3. *theáomai* – to behold and view attentively, indicating the sense of a wondering consideration involving a careful and deliberate vision which interprets its object. This is used once in the passage but is the same word used in John 1:14: "We have *seen* His glory..."

have *touched*[4] – this we proclaim concerning the Word of life. The life appeared; we have *seen* it and testify to it, and we proclaim to you the eternal life, which was with the Father and has appeared to us. We proclaim to you what we have *seen* and *heard*, so that you also may have fellowship with us. And our *fellowship*[5] is with the Father and with His Son, Jesus Christ. We write this to make our joy complete." (1 John 1:1-4)

Look again at the words John used: *heard, seen, looked at, touched* and *fellowship*. These are not only a description of John's experience, but the essence of the heart of the Lord who wants to be heard and seen and looked at and touched and shared with. The Incarnation was the Lord's ultimate and most radical expression in seeking a *face to face* with the people He created, wrestled with, spoke with and now lived among. When the Lord breathed into the first man at creation, there was nothing between His face and the man's, and this idea is captured in the heart of the first of God's Ten Words to His people when He asked:

"You shall have no other gods before Me." (Exodus 20:2)

A literal translation reads *"before My face"*.

Enshrined in this first Word is the heart of God to have a *face to face* relationship with those He loves; that nothing (god or otherwise) would get in-between His face and ours.

So, we return to Jacob and understand that the *face to face* encounter, though unique in experience, was not and is not unique in essence. The circumstances that brought Jacob to this *face to face* may reflect his journey alone, but the God at the heart of this story longs for a *face to face* with all those made in His image. As Jacob in humility and naked honesty struggled with God, with nothing in between them, the Lord finally had His son where He had always wanted him.

---

4. *psēlapháo¯* – to feel an object.
5. *koinōnía* – to share in or with, to participate with.

Decades before, Jacob had put another man's clothes and the skins of animals between himself and his blind father. Now, just as himself, he stood in a place of utter freedom, *face to face* with the One who named him and called him!

Why was *face to face* so important for Jacob and why should it be so important for us?

Face to Face brings revelation

Jacob's experience in Peniel is an echo of an earlier encounter at a place called Luz, renamed by Jacob as Bethel (*Bet'El* – house of God). We read about this from the beginning of Genesis 28 and it happens as Jacob hits the road into exile. (Take a moment to read the passage if you haven't already).

The connection to, and contrast with, Bethel and Peniel is another reason to understand that the latter is not a standalone event, but part of a wider context. What happened at Peniel demonstrates that Bethel may not have been the encounter that, on the surface, it appeared to be. It is not until we see both events side by side that we become aware just how different they are.

The first major tension between the two is in the area of revelation. Listen to Jacob's language in both. At Peniel he said:

"*I saw* God..." (Genesis 32:30)

Jacob saw the Lord for himself, recognising how fortunate he was to still be alive, having encountered God *face to face*. This was not a dream, an idea, or someone else's experience passed down to him; this was something Jacob saw for himself – and having truly seen Him, he could not un-see Him. Jacob didn't know the name of the person with whom he struggled and yet, he knew it was God! In a moment of revelation, he knew something that he did not learn or know before. *Jacob knew because he saw!*

At Bethel he said:

"Surely the Lord is in this place and *I was not aware of it.*" (Genesis 28:16)

Note the language, "is in this place" and "I was not aware" or *knew it not.* Jacob confessed to not knowing something that was right there in front of him. His dream suggested the Lord was there, but he did not *know* that because he could not *see* the Lord, thus he was unaware of Him. On the surface of it, Jacob seemed to encounter the Lord at Luz, but although he heard His voice in the dream, he did not see Him in the place. To reinforce this idea, listen to his conclusion:

"How awesome is this place!" (Genesis 28:17)

The place wasn't awesome, it was God who was awesome. But without truly seeing the Lord, the place becomes the focus of his response, believing it to be *Bet'El,* the house of God. Bethel could have been a transformational experience for Jacob, but here, instead of struggling, he accepts what has happened and moves on. What if Jacob had not simply accepted the fact that "he knew not" and pressed into the Lord at the top of the staircase? What if instead of declaring the place awesome, he had wrestled with the God who made it awesome? What if instead of just moving on, he had paused, reflected and taken hold of the Lord who was trying to get his attention? Jacob did none of these things because he was not aware and he did not see. Instead of a place of life-changing encounter, Bethel became a place to which many years later the Lord would call Jacob back, to finish what He started.

Jacob's experience in Bethel teaches us that it is possible to be in the "house of God" and yet miss the God of the house. If we are not careful, we settle for an experience without struggling into the encounter. In such scenarios, a place, *any place*, can quickly displace and replace Him. Bethel was an experience for Jacob whereas Peniel was an encounter. Bethel touched his mind, but Peniel impacted his heart. Bethel was a pit-stop on the road, while Peniel created a whole new pathway. Bethel was a place but Peniel was a Face!

In pursuit of our God-shaped identity and God-designed destiny, we must not settle for experience, for a cool place or a nice blessing on the road to wherever we are going – we must press in, push on, struggle for more of Him, so that we become aware and see Him with our own eyes. Someone once said that "good is the enemy of great", and Jacob calls to us to not allow the wonder of Bethel to distract us from the glory of Peniel. Had Jacob looked beyond the stairway and the angels, he would have seen the Lord, and that may have changed everything.

Face to Face creates relationship

Another tension within the comparison of Bethel and Peniel is in how the relationship between the Lord and Jacob is framed.

At Peniel he said:

"...I saw God face to face, *and yet my life was spared."* (Genesis 32:30)

His language reflected humility and gratitude for the grace and generosity of God, knowing that he had encountered God and had not been killed! Jacob now knew his place because he saw the Lord, and through the intimacy of his experience he knew something of what the Lord was like. Seeing the Lord *face to face* was very different from seeing Him from the bottom of a staircase.

At Bethel he said:

"*If God* will be with me and will watch over me on this journey I am taking and will give me food to eat and clothes to wear so that I return safely to my father's household, *then* the Lord will be my God and this stone that I have set up as a pillar will be God's house, and of all that You give me I will give You a tenth." (Genesis 28:20-22)

This is not the language of relationship, this the language of a business transaction! There is little humility here, very little gratitude, and no understanding of Who he is dealing with. Instead Jacob defaults to type and tries to do business with the Lord in the way he has done with people. Jacob was trying to make a deal with God, so rather than this becoming a moment of encounter, Bethel became for him just another moment of opportunity.

Look at the language of transaction:

"If God will be with me..."
"If God... will watch over me on this journey..."
"If God... food to eat and clothes to wear..."
"If God... (helps me to return), to my father's household..."
"...then... the Lord will be my God..."
"...then... this stone that I have set up as a pillar will be God's house..."
"...then... (of all that You give me), I will give a tenth."
'*If You* will ... *then I* will!'

Up to the Bethel moment there is no record of Jacob praying or engaging with God for himself. The only time he referred to God was in front of his father, when he used the Lord's name to deceive Isaac:
"The Lord *your* God gave me success." (Genesis 27:20)
His lack of awareness and knowledge of the Lord is revealed in the opportunism of his request at Bethel. Even having heard all the Lord had promised him (Genesis 28:13-15), he still tried to ensure that he had the upper hand and that God would do what he wanted!
Bethel and Peniel teach us that without relationship with the Lord, our engagement with Him can quickly become purely transactional in nature. It becomes about what we want, how He can help us, and how we can get Him to serve our purpose and desires. The Bethel experience sees God as an opportunity to be exploited, whereas Peniel sees the Lord as One to be served. Bethel interprets encounter purely for our benefit, whereas Peniel takes us to something bigger

than ourselves. Bethel says "This is what I want", whereas Peniel asks, "What do *You* want?" That's why *face to face* is vital for the discovery of our God-shaped identity and surrender to our God-designed destiny. Without *face to face* our pursuit of identity and destiny becomes purely about us; with encounter it becomes about Him.

Face to Face empowers reformation

Jacob's *face to face* with the Lord not only brought immediate change to both his name and literally his walk, but it set Jacob on a course to wholeness and ownership, ideas we'll pick up on in the last two chapters of this book. But the depth of the transformation that took place in him at Peniel is further understood when the Lord asked him to return once more to Bethel:

"Then God said to Jacob, 'Go up to Bethel and settle there, and build an altar to God, who appeared to you when you were fleeing from your brother Esau.'" (Genesis 35:1)

The contrast between Jacob's experience at Bethel *part 1* in chapter 28 and Bethel *part 2* in chapter 35 is so markedly different that it can only be explained and understood in the light of Peniel. Had his *face to face* at Peniel not happened, I am convinced that Bethel part 2 would never have been written. Let's look a little closer at what happened as he returned to Bethel.

Five things worthy of note from chapter 35:

It's by divine invitation
"Then God said to Jacob, 'Go up to Bethel…'" (v1)

Remember, the last time he came to Bethel it was because he was on the run.

It provoked some house cleaning
"Get rid of the foreign gods you have with you, and purify yourselves and change your clothes." (v2)

Back in Genesis 28, he made a promise to the Lord that he's now making good:

"...then the Lord will be my God..." (Genesis 28:21)

It connected the dots

"Then come, let us go up to Bethel, where I will build an altar to God, Who answered me in the day of my distress and Who has been with me wherever I have gone." (v3)

Looking back, he now sees the hand of God, guiding, directing, protecting and prospering. The grasper acknowledged that he owed his prosperity to the generosity of the Lord.

He built an altar

"There he built an altar..." (v7)

Back in Genesis 28 he set up a sort of stone pillar that marked the encounter moment, but now, having seen God face to face, he built an altar, a place of surrender and sacrifice. The stone of chapter 28 cost him nothing, in fact it wasn't even his, but the altar of chapter 35 was a mark of how seriously he took his relationship with the Lord and what He meant to him.

He saw the God of Bethel

"...and he called the place El Bethel." (v7)

Yet another naming ceremony, this time with the addition of God, making the place mean "God of Bethel". Could this be the final redemptive moment? Back in chapter 28 he said *the place* was *awesome* and called it Bethel. Now, having had a *face to face* with God, he understands *God is awesome*, thus changing the emphasis of the name from the place to the Person of the place!

Contrast his Bethel 2 experience to that of Bethel 1. After his dream encounter, the text matter-of-factly continues:

"Then Jacob continued on his journey and came to the land of the eastern peoples." (Genesis 29:1)

Reading this, it feels like nothing changed and Jacob just carried on as before. But if Jacob did not see the Lord for himself the first time at Bethel, then why would anything change? True, spiritual heart change only comes out of a revelation of the Lord and a relationship with Him, and Jacob's first experience at Bethel seems to reflect that neither were present. However, by the time the Lord invites him to return to Bethel, Peniel has happened and it is clear that the *face to face* of that night changed everything. *Peniel changed Bethel*! The Lord became the God of Bethel because a revelation of the Lord enabled relationship with Him; and relationship with Him empowered reformation for Him. All of this became possible because Jacob saw the Lord *face to face*.

It is interesting that the Prophet Hosea, when challenging the nation, refers to Jacob's experience:

"He struggled with the angel and overcame him; he wept and begged for his favour. He found him at Bethel and talked with him there." (Hosea 12:4)

Of which *Bethel* does Hosea speak?

Both from the order he placed it in the text and the implication of conversation, Hosea points to the second Bethel, that found in chapter 35. If that is the case, he makes no reference at all to Jacob's first Bethel experience. In chapter 28, the Lord talks *to* Jacob and Jacob talks *to* Him, but they do not talk together. However, in chapter 35 the text records:

"Then God went up from him at the place where He had talked *with* him." (v13)

In Bethel 1 Jacob talked *at* God, but in Bethel 2, having met with the Lord *face to face*, he talked *with* God.

Humans can and have changed themselves by sheer will-power and effort and I believe our ability to do so resides in the God-image within us. But spiritual reformation can only take place when we see the Lord and know His heart. If we are prepared to press beyond the excitement of Bethel and struggle with the God who wants to meet with us, then Peniel will change Bethel. The pursuit of a *face to face* relationship with the Lord will fuel a passion for Him, His people and His purpose. Without this, our spirituality is in danger of becoming superficial and transactional – an experience where love for a place eclipses a passion for Him. We need Peniel. We need a *face to face* engagement with God. This was how we were made; this was what we were designed for; and this is the only way we can truly live.

Our identity and destiny cannot be understood properly and completely outside of a *face to face* with the Lord. Without His face in our world, humanity is reduced down to a matter of biology, psychology and sociology. But when all of these are viewed through the lens of theology, everything changes. Understood within a Bible worldview, we cannot find our identity without Him, for to exclude the Lord from the conversation is to ensure we end up being less than who we are. Don't settle for an experience in His house, take hold of an encounter with His face.

Take a moment to reflect on the following questions:

Has a Bethel experience become a substitute for a face to face with the Lord?

If you were to describe how you have seen the Lord, how would you describe Him?

Chapter 11 – From Fugitive to Owner

Genesis 33:1-20

When the Lord asked Jacob to "Go back to the land" of his fathers,[1] the importance of that request was not merely its geographical significance, but its redemptive call to Jacob. The word translated "go back" in the NIV is *sŭḇ* and within its range of meaning lies not only to the idea of returning, but also restoration and restitution. Within the Hebrew Scriptures, this verb is at the heart of the concept of repentance, suggesting that as one *returns*, then restoration and renewal awaits! Jacob's call to go back was not simply a return to the land, but a journey that required him to turn back and face what he had originally run from. The Lord could only return and restore things to Jacob if he was willing to turn from where he was and return to where he was always meant to be. To go forward, Jacob had to go back and face the man he ran from, as well as the place he belonged and the promise he had received. He was being called to cast off the mantle of exile and embrace his God-shaped identity and God-designed destiny. He left as a fugitive, now he must return as an owner.

I have had the privilege of serving the Church full-time since the summer of 1987, and over the years I have observed three recurring mindsets that have influenced people as they have sought to follow Jesus and understand their place in both community and mission.

---

1. Genesis 31:3

8888888888

I confess that these observations are purely anecdotal, but in my experience they have been remarkably consistent.

The first mindset is *Squatter*

The dictionary defines a squatter as, "A person who unlawfully occupies an uninhabited building or unused land", and although the emphasis of the definition is to do with physical spaces, behind such action is a mentality that believes it is okay to take what isn't ours, or to reap the benefits of something for which we have neither worked nor paid for. The squatter sees what others have and what they have achieved and wants those things without making the sacrifices and investment necessary to make them happen. The squatter gets not by building but by taking. The squatter occupies not by right but by deceit. The squatter gains not by growth but by greed. The squatter is always looking for the easy option and the shortcut to success, hoping they can advance themselves through the achievements of others.

The spiritual squatter must learn that there are no shortcuts to anywhere worth going. Though we can benefit from the learning, life and love of others, we must not rely on that which trickles down to us, or claim something from them that we have never truly made our own. We must be careful not to squat in the spirituality of a family member, or the learning of a teacher, or in the abilities of a leader. It is so easy to feed off what is theirs while pretending it is ours, but to do so will leave us bankrupt, irrespective of any short-term gain.

Paul urged the church at Corinth to:

"Follow my example, as I follow the example of Christ." (1 Corinthians 11:1)

He said something similar earlier in the letter when he wrote,

"Therefore, I urge you to imitate me." (1 Corinthians 4:16)

The word translated *example* and *imitate* are exactly the same in both verses: *mimeīes̄*. Together they show us that Paul is not merely calling for the Corinthian believers to copy him, but to see him as an example of one following Jesus, thus showing them what it looks like.[2] They are not to be mini-Pauls, squatting on his experience, but rather they are to learn from him, they are to create and embrace their own experience. They are being called to follow, not fake!

On the surface, the benefits of squatting are impressive, but when probed and put under pressure, they reveal nothing of substance. Don't squat in a false identity or in the achievements of someone else's house, have the courage to own who you are, where you are and what you have.

The second mindset is *Renter*

A renter is someone who occupies a house, building or space legally, with the understanding that what they occupy and pay for belongs to someone else. Every landlord hopes that their tenant has an "owner" mentality when living in their property, while accepting that the tenant is obliged to do only what the law and/or the contract requires. The renter lives in a space they do not own and therefore must resolve how they behave towards the property. Do they do "just enough" or do they treat what belongs to someone else as if it were theirs? Many, of course, will choose the latter option, but most will opt for the former.

So often I have encountered a *just enough* mindset when it comes to our attitude to the Lord, His called-out community and His passion for the world. But we must remember that although *just enough* is legal, it's not life-giving! Our contribution is as much about our own heart's wellbeing as it is about benefitting the context we occupy. When we give, we grow. But when we hide behind *just enough*, we miss an opportunity to go beyond ourselves, beyond what is required into something that blesses others and enlarges us.

---

2. Paul also uses the same word and idea in Eph.5:1, 1 Thess.1:6 and 2:14. It's used again in Hebrews 6:12 and 1 Peter 3:13

Proverbs speaks into this very idea:

"One person gives freely, yet gains even more;
another withholds unduly, but comes to poverty.
A generous person will prosper;
whoever refreshes others will be refreshed.
People curse the one who hoards grain,
but they pray God's blessing on the one who is willing to sell."
(Proverbs 11:24-26)

The proverb is not teaching us that it is wrong to withhold, for in other parts of the same book the listener is encouraged to save and store. Rather, the mentality being challenged here is to "withhold unduly" or *hold back more than we should*. We will never be enlarged by a *just enough* mentality, instead it will only shrink us. *Just enough* is legal, but it's not life-giving! On the surface of it *just enough* is enough, but for the God who surrendered everything for us, it will never be enough.

The third mindset is *Owner*

My first ministry opportunity after leaving Bible College was to lead a lovely but small group of people in a little village in Yorkshire, England. It was an amazing privilege and I will be forever grateful to that handful of saints who gave, served and believed in the most challenging of circumstances. The village only had approximately 2,000 residents and most of the homes were rented either to the British Coal Board or the Council. During our time there we saw a social transformation take place in the area. I would love to tell you it was because of the anointing of their dynamic young leader or the spiritual revival that swept through the area. But the key to the transformation was ownership. A scheme was launched by the government to encourage greater home ownership and an incredible opportunity was created for those who had perhaps rented homes all their lives to now own their space. Many people took up the offer and with it, mentalities were changed from *just enough* to *whatever it takes*. The space the people lived in was exactly the same, but the mindset of the people living in the space was revolutionised! That experience taught me a life-changing lesson: *ownership changes everything.*

Great enterprises are not built by squatters or renters, they are built and established by owners; by ordinary people who understand that anything of value and substance will cost and require from them something of greatness, grit and generosity. Owners embrace their responsibility to do whatever it takes, understanding that *just enough* will get us so far, but not all the way. Owners aren't deterred by squatters or distracted by renters, but commit themselves to *doing*, even if others can't, don't or won't.

Barnabas was an owner:

"Joseph, a Levite from Cyprus, whom the apostles called Barnabas (which means 'son of encouragement'), sold a field he owned and brought the money and put it at the apostles' feet."

(Acts 4:36)

This statement comes at the end of Acts chapter 4 and is in direct contrast to the events of the first part of chapter 5, where Ananias and Sapphira also sold property but kept part of the money back (something they were entitled to do). For them, the issue wasn't about keeping some of the money, but lying about the fact. Their *just enough* mentality was exposed and they paid a high price for their behaviour. Compare that to Joseph, now called Barnabas, who moved beyond *just enough* into *whatever it takes*! Side by side, both episodes are remembered and both mindsets are highlighted to show the power of authentic ownership and the tyranny of spiritual pretence. *Ownership changes everything!*

Jacob's experience in some ways represents the journey from squatter to owner.

When Jacob said, "I am Esau..." he squatted in the rights of his brother, taking a name, clothes and a position that did not belong to him. While Esau was out, Jacob moved in and took full advantage of his brother's vacated space. However, he discovered that the short-term gain soon gave way to significant loss and pain!

When working for Laban, Jacob toiled in another man's house and worked for another man's success. Though deceived, used and abused, Jacob had to wrestle with the temptation to do *just enough*, overcoming the shock of Leah and the unscrupulous behaviour of Laban. Yet, the text suggests he did just that, and moved from being a renter to live as an owner in his uncle's world:

"You know that I've worked for your father with all my strength, yet your father has cheated me by changing my wages ten times. However, God has not allowed him to harm me." (Genesis 31:6-7)

It could be argued that Laban *squatted* on Jacob, but the grasper learned to rise above such smallness and experienced the ability of the Lord to enlarge his world, even when others were trying to shrink it. Jacob left Laban as an owner, but this ownership had little to do with his flocks and herds and the size of his family. The young man who fled as a squatter and lived as a renter, returned with the mindset of an owner, wrestling with God Himself for something he was beginning to understand and truly believe in. Having come *face to face* with the Lord, Jacob, Israel, was ready to come *face to face* with his past, the place and the promise.

He took ownership of the Past

"Jacob looked up and there was Esau..." (Genesis 33:1)

The last recorded words spoken by Esau about Jacob before he left for Paddan Aram were to himself, but somehow the message got out:

"The days of mourning for my father are near; then I will kill my brother Jacob." (Genesis 27:41)

This was the last thing Jacob heard his brother say about him and with that thought bouncing around in his mind he fled. Though decades had passed, Jacob understood that he could not go back to the land and go forward with his purpose without facing his brother. Some things can't be ignored. This could not! As Jacob approached Esau, both his behaviour and language are worthy of note:

"He himself went on ahead and bowed down to the ground seven times as he approached his brother." (Genesis 33:3)

The nuance of the word translated "bowed" here might point to either a respectful bow or even an act of prostration. If the latter, the fact that Jacob does it seven times shows the seriousness with which he took this moment. Knowing Jacob's track record, we might be tempted to conclude that this is just another one of his games. After all, he knew how to play the system and understood such a public demonstration would be hard to ignore. But this conclusion, though understandable, would need to ignore Jacob's encounter with the Lord, which had a significant impact on him and is reflected in his language to Esau:

"'For to see your face is like seeing the face of God, now that you have received me favourably. Please accept the present that was brought to you, for God has been gracious to me and I have all I need.' And because Jacob insisted, Esau accepted it." (Genesis 33:10-11)

We've alluded in a previous chapter to the fact that "the present", as the NIV translates it, might refer to the *blessing* Jacob stole from his brother. But having examined Jacob's *face to face* encounter with the Lord, we cannot ignore the reference to Esau's *face* being like the *face of God*. In what sense? Look how Jacob concluded his words to Esau:

"…now that you have received me favourably."

Remember, Jacob claimed that he saw God *face to face* and yet *his life was spared* (Genesis 32:30), thus concluding the Lord had accepted him. Now he faced Esau and again *his life was spared*. Having been favourably received by his brother, Jacob likens this to seeing the face of God again. This is not pretence on Jacob's part, or another example of the grasper manipulating his brother, but rather his actions and words are an authentic expression of a changed man. As Jacob had faced the Lord with humility and naked honesty, so the same attributes are present when he meets Esau – and from both the Lord and Esau he got the same response: favour and acceptance.

The Lord wants each of us to live with our eyes looking forward, not to be forever glancing fearfully over our shoulder at what might be lurking in the past. His redemptive purpose for us is one that includes not only the forgiveness of our past, but the power of learning from it and living beyond it. But there are times when, even though our past is forgiven, it must still be faced and addressed. This will not be everyone's experience, but for some of us there are issues that cannot be ignored; which must be resolved so that we can move forward into our future. Over the years I've heard people say, "the past is the past", but in some cases it's not. An unresolved past is not in the past, it tends to bleed into the present and threaten the future.

Zacchaeus intuitively understood this. When the Lord revolutionised his world by stepping into his home, Zacchaeus knew he could not simply move on by consigning the past to the past. He knew he had to take ownership for what he had done, face it, resolve it as far as he could, then move on from it:

"Look, Lord! Here and now I give half of my possessions to the poor, and if I have cheated anybody out of anything, I will pay back four times the amount." (Luke 19:8)

Presented with an opportunity to move forward by the Lord, both Jacob and Zacchaeus realised the past had to be faced, as might be the case for some of us. Redemption sometimes calls for restitution and even reconciliation, but it will always ask us to face and own what has been, so that what has been does not derail what will be.

Take a moment to reflect:

Is there anything in your past that is threatening your future?

Is it something you can address and resolve?

Is it worth facing what has been, so that it does not derail what will be?

He took ownership of the Place

If we didn't know better, chapter 33 looks like the reunion of two close friends making up for lost time. It is Esau who makes the suggestion that Jacob and his family travel with him back to Seir, but Jacob tactfully and firmly manages to resist the offer. Not only that, but he also persuades Esau not to leave any of his men with him.

The Torah then summarises the next moment beautifully:

"So that day Esau started on his way back to Seir. Jacob however, went to Succoth." (Genesis 33:16-17)

What seems like a routine piece of information is deeply significant. If we look at a map of the land of Canaan at that time, Peniel, where Jacob encountered the Lord, lay east of the Jordan near the Jabbok River, while the northern border of Seir was approximately 100 miles further south of this point, east of the Dead Sea. To go with Esau would have meant taking Jacob away from the land of his father and grandfather, not towards it. Jacob makes a bold but strategic decision, (one that might have incurred the wrath of his brother), not to go south, but to go west, across the Jordan to Succoth and then on to Shechem. To go south was to go away from the land, but to go west was to go into the land. Jacob's decision was not random, selfish or even pragmatic – this was to do with place and purpose. Having once run from the land of promise, he was now determined to return no matter what.

Again, his journey to Shechem was not coincidental, but deeply intentional. Jacob was grasping a golden thread that originated from there many years before with his grandfather Abraham:

"Abram travelled through the land as far as the site of the great tree of Moreh at Shechem. At that time the Canaanites were in the land. The Lord appeared to Abram and said, 'To your offspring I will give this land.' So he built an altar there to the Lord, who had appeared to him." (Genesis 12:6-7)

Shechem was the first place Abram stopped when he arrived in the place the Lord had sent him. The Lord spoke to him and reinforced the promise that his offspring would have the land and, finally, he built an altar there. It cannot be a coincidence that Jacob, on returning to the land, having heard the Lord speak and then encountering Him face to face, made his way to the place where his grandfather met with God, received a promise and built an altar. His journey to Shechem was a declaration of ownership over the land that had played, and would play, such a huge role in the purpose of God.

Life-giving ownership happens when what He wants becomes what we want; where our decisions are not based on what is best for us, or on what is obvious or expected. Instead, we go where He wants us to go, regardless of the result or the reaction. Expediency, pragmatism and human wisdom will sometimes say "go south", but the Lord's compass will always be set to take us into *His place* and purpose, never away from it.

Solomon instructs us:
"Trust in the Lord with all your heart
and lean not on your own understanding;
in all your ways acknowledge Him,
and He will make your paths straight." (Proverbs 3:5-6)

The word translated "acknowledge" here is *yāḏa'* and at its simplest means "to know, perceive and learn". To acknowledge in this context means that we come to know, understand and perceive what the Lord actually wants, and from this our paths will be straight. The straightness of our paths depends on knowing what He wants! Too often we pick a path that we want the Lord to acknowledge, in the hope that He'll still make it straight. But if we want to walk in the freedom of our God-shaped identity and our God-designed destiny, then we must come to know His way and choose to walk in it.

Take a moment to reflect:

Are you willing to seek to acknowledge His way for you?

Are you willing to surrender your right to choose south and allow Him to pick the route?

He took ownership of the Promise

As we draw near to the end of chapter 33, we are confronted with a remarkable fact:

"For a hundred pieces of silver, he bought from the sons of Hamor, the father of Shechem, the plot of ground where he pitched his tent." (Genesis 33:19)

But why should Jacob buy land that he could claim the Lord had promised was his?

This is Jacob's first purchase in the land, and so often in the Scriptures the first mention of something can be significant. Just as Shechem became the place of Abram's first encounter with God and his first altar, so now it becomes the place of Jacob's first purchase. Jacob put his own money on the table (we're not sure what value 100 pieces of silver equates to, but it sounds like a lot), and in that first purchase he took ownership of the promise the Lord originally made there to his grandfather:

"To your offspring I will give this land." (Genesis 12:7)

Jacob was that offspring. He was taking ownership of the promise.

In buying the land he took ownership of the promise the Lord made to his father:

"I will make your descendants as numerous as the stars in the sky and will give them all these lands, and through your offspring all nations on earth will be blessed…" (Genesis 26:4)

Jacob was that offspring. He was taking ownership of the promise.

In buying the land he took ownership of the promise the Lord gave to him:

"I am the Lord, the God of your father Abraham and the God of Isaac. I will give you and your descendants the land on which you are lying." (Genesis 28:13)

Jacob was that descendant and now had descendants of his own. He was taking ownership of the promise.

As Abraham had bought land,[3] so his grandson Jacob followed suit and, hundreds of years later, his descendants would literally reap the benefits of his purchase:

"And Joseph's bones, which the Israelites had brought up from Egypt, were buried at Shechem in the tract of land that Jacob bought for a hundred pieces of silver from the sons of Hamor, the father of Shechem. This became the inheritance of Joseph's descendants." (Joshua 24:32)[4]

Between purchasing the land and Joseph's bones being buried there, Jacob's family had settled in Egypt. They had become slaves and Moses had led them to freedom and nationhood. The Law was given, the Tabernacle established and, after a generation of wandering in the wilderness, the Land of Promise was in the process of being

---

3. Genesis 23:1-20

4. Before Jacob died, he asked to be buried not in Egypt, but the land purchased by Abraham (Genesis 49:29-33). Perhaps this inspired Joseph's request for burial and provides another beautiful moment of symmetry in the text.

retaken. But even though they entered the land as conquerors under Joshua, there was no dispute over this piece of land, because Jacob had bought it and now his descendants legally owned it! Jacob's first purchase didn't just align him with the promises of the past, but set up a living legacy for generations to come. He so believed in the promise that he was prepared to invest himself and his wealth into it, knowing a people yet to be born would reap the benefits.

The journey to ownership will ultimately require not just the submission of our minds in acknowledging what the Lord wants, but the surrender of our resources to enable that to happen. The Lord we serve is the Creator of the Universe and He owns everything within it. As such He could write any cheque and supply the means for every scheme and plan. But the Scriptures show us that the Lord leaves room for our contribution, not because He can't supply but because we must learn to invest. It was Thomas Paine who said, "What we obtain too cheap we esteem too lightly, it is dearness only that gives everything its value."[5]

Whatever journey we are on, the Lord will never supply everything for the task. Instead, He will always leave room for ownership to arise, creating opportunities for His people to sacrifice, invest and spend for a cause beyond themselves. Even the promises the Lord has given us will often require ownership from us in order to teach us the value of what is and what will be.

Take a moment to reflect:

Are you expecting the Lord to meet every need in regard to His promise to you?

---

5. *The American Crisis* is a collection of articles written by Thomas Paine during the American Revolutionary War in 1776. This quote is from *Common Sense*, an extremely popular and successful pamphlet arguing for independence from England.

What are you prepared to invest into the promise to show your ownership of it?

If the promise is not just about today, but about leaving a legacy for the future, would that change how and what you invest in today?

Ownership changes everything. When we are prepared to take ownership of our God-shaped identity and invest into our God-designed destiny we make room for a spectacular partnership to emerge – one where the greatness and glory of the Lord is manifest in the weakness and limitation of our humanity.

Chapter 12 – From Your God to My God

Genesis 33:20

Though the conclusion of chapter 33 is not the end of Jacob's story, it is a fitting end to our journey with him. Jacob was "gathered to his people" at the age of 147, surrounded by his family, while living in Egypt. But this moment, captured for us in the final verse of the chapter, is for me a gloriously climatic finale.[1] The baby born grasping for himself is now transformed into a man surrendered in worship unto God. Having bought the land in Shechem that his tent was pitched on, his first recorded action on his newly acquired real estate was not to build a house for himself, but an altar for the Lord. If we doubted the extent of the change within him, this moment settles our concerns, for as we observe Jacob before the altar, we see a man at rest, at ease with himself and his God. No longer a fugitive or a foreigner, Jacob is home and he is whole! The Torah sums up this sacred event in eight magnificent words (in Hebrew):

"There he set up an altar and called it El Elohe Israel." (Genesis 33:20)

Beyond the border of this chapter, challenges, trials, heartache, joys and sorrows await the great man and his family, but before we rush into the next episode, we are encouraged to pause, reflect, slow down and look closely at one of the most significant moments in Jacob's life. He returned from exile, emerged from the garden and survived a reunion with his brother.

---

1. Genesis 47:28

Now, on a piece of promised land, purchased with his own money, we witness a sacred event. This simple sentence represents three transformational *firsts* for Jacob. It is the first altar he built; it is the first time we hear him refer to God as *his* God; and it is the first time he used the name Israel as his own name. Add to this the fact that all of this took place on land he bought as his first purchase, and we get the sense that this is the dawning of a new day for Adonai's grasping son.

Let's take a closer look at these three firsts.

He built an altar

"There he set up *an altar…*"

The word translated "altar" is *mizbēaḥ* and is used for altar in the Old Testament/Tanakh in all but four references. The root of this word is the verb *zāḇaḥ*, which means "to slaughter, kill or sacrifice", thus the idea of this *mizbēaḥ altar* is synonymous with sacrifice. It's this truth that distinguishes Jacob's memorial pillar of Bethel from his altar at Shechem,[2] for while the pillar was cheap and easy, the altar was costly and expensive.

Altars were part of the world of his grandfather and father. Abraham built four altars at Shechem, between Bethel and Ai, at Hebron and Moriah, while Isaac built only one altar at Beersheba.[3] Jacob built two, the first here at Shechem and the second when he returned to Bethel. However, the difference between these two altars is worthy of note, as his second at Bethel was built at the request of the Lord, whereas this one was built from his own initiative and desire.[4] Jacob did not build an altar because his fathers did, rather he built an altar for himself, out of a *face to face* encounter with the God who changed him and now shapes him.

2. Genesis 28:18
3. Abraham's altars: Genesis 12:6-8, 13:18 and 22:9. Isaac's altar: Genesis 26:25
4. Bethel altar details are found in Genesis 35:1-15

The altar was important because it represented two huge ideas, namely those of *worship* and *worth*. In building an altar to the Lord, Jacob acknowledged the Lord as God. The prominent, visible position of the altar was a reminder of the centrality of His presence. The altar was not his focus, but rather the God for whom it was built! But, of course, by design an altar must have something placed upon it, and this symbolised the idea of worth. Later, through the Law, the Lord would regulate what worth looked like through the instigation of the Levitical sacrificial system. But what He always longed for were worshippers – those who would see His worth for themselves and bring an offering worthy of His glory.

The essence of this idea is captured in the story that led up to the first murder in the Torah. Two brothers, Cain and Abel, without being asked, brought their offerings to the Lord. We are told that Cain brought "...the fruits of the soil as an offering to the Lord..." while Abel brought "...fat portions from some of the firstborn of his flock." The Lord's reaction to their offerings was diverse:

"The Lord looked with favour on Abel and his offering, but on Cain and his offering he did not look with favour."

However, it is Cain's reaction that is deeply puzzling:

"So Cain was very angry, and his face was downcast."[5]

Why didn't Cain ask *why*? Even in the very next verse, when the Lord challenged him to do "what is right" he doesn't ask *why*! Cain's offering was not rejected because of what it was, it was rejected because of how it was brought. The fact that Cain didn't ask why means that, deep down, he didn't care about the feelings, desires or wants of the God he brought the offering to. Somehow *by faith*, Abel offered a better sacrifice – not in substance, but in attitude – and the Lord accepted what he brought because of the way he brought it. Abel understood the *worth* of the One he was dealing with, whereas for Cain, it was just an offering!

---

5. Genesis 4:1-7 (though it is worth reading the whole chapter)

The altar can be a place of *lust* or *love*, and on the surface, both can look the same. Lust (in whatever arena it arises) is about what we can get. Therefore, any act of generosity we make is not about the person we express it to, it's purely about what we hope to get back from them. Lust can look like love, but it is deeply selfish with the focus firmly on the person/object that can give us what we want. Love, on the other hand, is about what we can give to enrich, encourage and bless the object of our giving with no conditions. With love, there are no strings attached to the gift – it is given freely and without condition.

As we observe Cain and Abel, we see the same contrast in behaviour, but clearly from the reaction of the Lord, something else is going on. Dare I say that Cain came with lust in his heart and wanted something from God, whereas Abel came in love and gave something to God? This very idea was reflected in Jacob's experience. As alluded to in a previous chapter, at Bethel he sought to make a deal with God praying, "If You will… then I…" With such a mentality of lust, it was no surprise that a pillar was erected, not an altar. But now at Shechem there are no deals, no ifs and then. Instead, at the altar of Shechem we have love; a gift given without strings and worship given without conditions.

Today, because of the sacrifice of Jesus on the altar of Calvary, we no longer need to build physical altars and offer animal sacrifices, but the ideas contained within the altar remain at the heart of our relationship with the Lord. He is looking for a people who, in worship, will place Him at the centre of everything and allow Him to be the God of all. He longs for a people who understand Who He is and will bring the best they have to Him. The Lord doesn't want our lust, He longs for our love. The Lord doesn't want to be used, He longs to be worshipped. The Lord doesn't want pillars and bargains, He wants altars and blessing. An altar mentality says, He alone is worth it and He is worthy of the best we are, and have!

Take a moment to reflect:

How much of your worship is actually about Him, and how much of it is about you?

Have you settled the idea that He deserves your best in all things, or is this still an issue of negotiation?

He made an agreement

"...and called it *El Elohe* Israel."

Translated this means *God, the God of...* and in this context He is the God of Jacob (although he used the name Israel, but we'll get to that next). This is the first time Jacob referred to God as *his* God. The text up to this point shows Jacob talking about God, but not in a deeply personal way. Look at these examples:

"Then Jacob made a vow, saying, 'If God will be with me... then the Lord will be my God.'"

(Genesis 28:20-21)

"...but the God of my father has been with me." (Genesis 31:5)

"If the God of my father, the God of Abraham and the Fear of Isaac, had not been with me..." (Genesis 31:42)

"Then Jacob prayed, 'O God of my father Abraham, God of my father Isaac...'" (Genesis 32:9)

All of these point to an understanding of God, and within the context of cultural norms, a respect of and identification with God. But nowhere does Jacob refer to the Lord as *his* God. However, the naming of the altar at Shechem brings to our ears the echo of a statement Jacob made before his blind and aged father all those years ago. When asked by his father how he had managed to accomplish the task so quickly, Jacob replied:

"The Lord *your* God gave me success." (Genesis 27:20)

Perhaps Jacob had helped his father build his altar at Beersheba and had been impacted by Isaac's quiet and relentless faith. But by the time he steals the *blessing*, Isaac's God is not his God – at least not by way of revelation and personal engagement. Having lied so shamefully all those years ago and used his father's God to get what he wanted, surely it can be no coincidence that the name he gave to God at his first altar was, "God, the God of Israel." Though he had been in covenant with God by circumcision, he was now in covenant by heart. A cut on his body that seemed to mean so little became a cut in his heart that now meant everything. Because of his *face to face* encounter, the Lord had gone from "God of my father" to "my God".

What is beautiful is that, hundreds of years later, the Lord found a shepherd looking after his flocks at the back end of a desert. He got the attention of Moses by calling to him from flames of fire from within a bush. As Moses approached, the Lord introduced Himself:

"I am the God of your father, the God of Abraham, the God of Isaac and the God of Jacob." (Exodus 3:6)

Forever, He would be known as the God of Abraham, Isaac *and Jacob*, because He was the God of all three. All three men knew Him, walked with Him and built altars to Him. The altar at Shechem secured Jacob's name in the Divine introduction!

There is a glorious tension within the pilgrimage of faith revealed in the fact that the Lord is *our* God. He is God of a people and a called-out community, but He also wants to be *my* God. What we recite in *corporate confession* He wants us to know by *personal revelation*. The Lord of *many* is also the Lord of *one* and still seeks to be known in such a way. The Gospel of John records for us a transformational moment when Thomas, one of Jesus' young disciples, saw Him for himself and declared:

"*My* Lord and *my* God." (John 20:28)

John tells us that a week before, Jesus had appeared to the disciples while Thomas (it had to be him) was absent. When Thomas returned they said to him,

"*We* have seen the Lord." (John 20:25)

Thomas knew that whatever they had seen, it was not enough for him. They could bless him and encourage him out of the revelation they'd had, but if he was to live, serve and go for Jesus, then he needed a revelation for himself. Thomas knew he could not worship off another's wonder; he could not survive off someone else's revelation. If he was to go, he needed to get Jesus for himself.

Whatever our fathers and mothers have in the Lord is not enough for us – we must have Him for ourselves.

Whatever our spouse believes is not enough for us – we must believe for ourselves.

Whatever our spiritual leaders understand is not enough for us – we must know for ourselves.

Only when we can declare with clarity, *El Elohe...* (insert your name) will we be able to go with confidence and authority, knowing that wherever we are and whatever life throws at us, He is not only *our* God, but *my* God!

Take a moment to reflect:

What truth that you have seen for yourself could you declare with confidence?

Is there any area of your life where you are trying to live off someone else's revelation?

Make it daily prayer that the Lord would open your eyes to see for yourself.

He embraced a name

"...and called it El Elohe *Israel.*"

It is one thing to be given a name, it is another to take it. Jacob was given this name by the Lord when they wrestled, but this is the first time he used it for himself. By embracing the name and taking it as his own, he not only acknowledged the authority of the Lord to give the name to him, but he surrendered to the meaning and purpose of the name itself. This name was more than a label or a signal of a change of character – this was the Lord placing a claim of ownership on Jacob; calling him to let go of his own ideas and agenda and to walk in submission to the Lord's. Just as others had named him Jacob because they observed a grasping baby, so the Lord called out what He saw and with it, all that Jacob could become. The nation that came from Jacob would eventually take his new name, but only if he embraced it first and accepted it as his own.

In order to embrace Israel as his own, Jacob had to address two strongholds within his own world:

Firstly, *how others saw him.*

This is summed up so powerfully in the words of Esau that we considered earlier, and it's worth reminding ourselves of them in this context:

"Isn't he rightly named Jacob?" (Genesis 27:36)

This wasn't a compliment from Esau but a barbed criticism. He more than anyone had experienced the rough end of Jacob's personality and abilities. Esau concluded that his brother was living up to his name and this would always be his lot.

This is echoed years later when Jacob is serving his uncle Laban. In order to keep Jacob from leaving, Laban struck an agreement with him over the management of their livestock. As a result of Jacob's ingenuity, the Torah tells us that the weak animals went to Laban and the strong ones to Jacob, thus ensuring he prospered more than his uncle. Laban's sons were not happy and concluded,

"Jacob has taken everything our father owned and has gained all this wealth from what belonged to our father." (Genesis 31:1)

By using the word *lāqaḥ*, translated here as "taken", the sons were undoubtedly making a play on Jacob's name, just as Esau did in Genesis 31:36, when he used the word twice:

"He *took* my birthright, and now he's *taken* my blessing!"

Depending on the context, this word can point to grasping for something, or even taking it by force. Clearly, just as Esau had concluded, Laban's sons also believed Jacob was living up to his name. As Jacob heard the name Israel spoken over him, however, he heard a view of himself expressed that he had never heard before – and the Lord's view of him seemed to be significantly different. If God's voice was to be heard and his name embraced, then the voices of Esau and the sons of Laban had to be silenced!

As the Lord calls us into our God-shaped identity and God-designed destiny, it will demand that we embrace His view of us, regardless and in spite of the views of others. He wants to rename us (in some cases that may be literal) according to our redeemed image in Christ Jesus, and for the purpose which accompanies that name. However, the Lord's voice, though clear, strong and truth-filled has to contend with other voices in our heads and our experience. These voices may have come from people we love and respect, or from people we never want to see again, but they live in us and influence us.

This truth is dramatically illustrated in a later event in the life of Jacob. Rachel, the love of his life, gave birth to their second son, Jacob's twelfth in all, but tragically she died in childbirth. As she was dying, Rachel named the child *ben 'ôniy*, and although there is some ambiguity around the meaning, it is generally accepted to mean, *son of my sorrow*. Rachel named what she saw, for the baby had brought her sorrow and death. However, at that moment, as Rachel passed, Jacob renamed the boy *binyāmiyn*, meaning *son of my right hand*, and by inference, *son of my strength*. Two people saw the same baby but concluded different things; one saw sorrow and the other strength. I'm glad (as I'm sure Benjamin was) that Jacob's view won the day!

Those who named us believed that what they saw was true, but *Israel* demonstrates to us that it is neither the whole truth nor the final truth. Just as Jacob renamed Ben-Oni, and the Lord renamed Jacob, so part of God's redemptive purpose for each of His children is for our identity to be rooted in, and grow out of, what He says about us and how He sees us. He calls us, therefore, to let His voice become our confession and His view of us become our vision.

Secondly, *how he saw himself.*

Our view of self can hinder what the Lord wants to achieve in our lives, either because we create an image so inflated that we do not want the Lord, or one so deflated that we conclude the Lord would not want us. Jacob's self-sufficiency and his inflated view of himself runs as a constant theme through his story. So much of what he does, he does without consulting or engaging with the Lord. Though he acknowledged God's blessing in his life, the Lord was very much a bit player in the Jacob show. This was why a *face to face* with the Lord was so crucial in his transformation. For the first time in his life he realised he could not do it alone, and encountered *Someone* who could not be manipulated, outmanoeuvred or overpowered. The once proud Jacob who ran from his brother and his father's house in his own strength, limped from the garden after meeting the Lord – every step a reminder that there was One greater than him.

One of the most challenging journeys of our lives is moving from how we see ourselves to how the Lord sees us. Any view of self, whatever it may be, that is not rooted in the truth of how the Lord sees us, is a potential obstacle that might prevent *Israel* living through us. If we can accept *we are who He says we are,* allowing that truth to override who *we* think we are, or who others have said we are, a life far from pretence and disguise awaits; a life of freedom, fuelled by the truth of His Word and the power of His grace. Imagine if we could hear these words and truly believe them:

"But now, this is what the Lord says –
He who created you, Jacob,
He who formed you, Israel:
'Do not fear, for I have redeemed you;
I have summoned you by name; you are Mine.'" (Isaiah 43:1)

What if we believed what *the Lord said to us*?
What if we rejoiced that *He created us*?
What if we accepted that *He formed us*?
What if we understood what *being redeemed by Him* really meant?
What if we embraced the fact that *we are His*?

Take a moment to reflect:

Why not create a confession out of Isaiah 43:1?

"The Word of the Lord to me is true. He created me, formed me, redeemed me and I am His."

Why not take other great statements of truth the Lord makes about you in the context of His redeemed community and create some life-giving confessions from the God-breathed Word. (Ephesians 2:10 is a good starting point).

As he moved towards the place of his first altar, the Torah records:

"…he arrived safely at the city of Shechem." (Genesis 33:18)

Many versions of the Bible translate *Vayavo Ya'akov shalem* as "…and Jacob came safely…" (ESV), "…he arrived safely…" (NIV) or "…and Jacob came in peace…" (JPS). But Rabbi Jonathan Sacks ventures another possible interpretation. Pointing to the fact that *šālēm* has a range of meanings such as safe, whole, peaceful and complete, he suggests that Jacob "…emerged complete…" and that this was "…the stunning truth at which Jacob finally arrived…"[6]

---

6. Rabbi Jonathan Sacks, *Covenant and Conversation: Genesis*, Maggid Books, UK, 2009, p.227

I love the idea that the baby born grasping, the young man manipulating, the schemer with another man's name, and the fugitive on the run, eventually – because of a *face to face* encounter with the Living God – arrived complete and whole, at rest in himself and at peace with the Lord. As he stood before the altar he did so without pretence and disguise, offering up his worship and able to say in freedom and confidence, "El Elohe Israel."

We too can arrive complete, if in humility, hunger and honesty we position ourselves before the Lord, *face to face*. The tyranny of pretence will leave us exhausted, frustrated and disappointed, as we attempt to sustain the person we were never meant to be. But if we will have the courage to let go of *Esau* and take hold of the Lord, then the Lord can take hold of *Jacob* and release the *Israel* within us to the world!

> "The nations will see your righteousness,
> and all kings your glory;
> you will be called by a new name
> that the mouth of the Lord will bestow."
> (Isaiah 62:2)

Printed in Poland
by Amazon Fulfillment
Poland Sp. z o.o., Wrocław

17705003R00097